Constructing A LIFE PHILOSOPHY

AN EXAMINATION OF ALTERNATIVES

DAVID L. BENDER
Editor

GREENHAVEN PRESS — ANOKA, MINNESOTA 55303

New, revised and extended edition

© COPYRIGHT 1971, 1973 by GREENHAVEN PRESS

ISBN 0-912616-10-5 PAPER EDITION
ISBN 0-912616-28-8 CLOTH EDITION

TABLE OF CONTENTS

TABLE OF EXERCISES

A major emphasis of this book is on critical thinking skills. Discussion exercises included after readings are not laborious writing assignments. They are written only to stimulate class discussion and individual critical thinking.

Men enjoy a great number of blessings in consequence of knowing themselves, and incur a great number of evils, through being deceived in themselves. For they who know themselves know what is suitable for them, and distinguish between what they can do and what they cannot; and, by doing what they know how to do, procure for themselves what they need, and are prosperous, and, by abstaining from what they do not know, live blamelessly, and avoid being unfortunate. By this knowledge of themselves, too, they can form an opinion of other men, and, by their experience of the rest of mankind, obtain for themselves what is good, and guard against what is evil.

SOCRATES

WHO ARE YOU?

In our pluralistic culture, with competing religions, value systems, political ideologies and life styles, young people and others are confronted with confusing choices. To what should they commit themselves? What life philosophy, world view or value system should they choose?

Prominent educators, church leaders, politicians and professional people have commented on our need for a life directing guidance system:

> *I spend a lot of time at colleges and universities, and I can tell you that one of the gut issues today on campus is the search for reality: "Where did I come from? Why am I here? Where am I going?" Modern education is not answering these questions that burn in the hearts of millions of students in America and throughout the world.*
>
> **Rev. Billy Graham** [1]

> *There is a deepening awareness that today's domestic turbulence is in reality a fundamental questioning of the value system of American society. . . . The widespread student antagonism toward the standards of "the establishment" represents an even broader disagreement with conventional values.*
>
> **Stewart Udall** [2]

> *Where am I going? What should I strive to become? Whenever we ask "What is the meaning of life?" what we want to know is the meaning of our own individual life. As far as I know, this last is something to which all men everywhere feel either that they have an answer or that they are in need of one. We rarely find men content with no*

[1] Billy Graham, *Three American Illusions,* **Christianity Today**, December 19, 1969, p. 13.

[2] Stewart Udall, *The Value Revolution: New Directions for Society?* **The Minneapolis Tribune**, June 23, 1969.

answer; and when we do, they no longer care much about anything, including life. They are men without purpose.

Ward H. Goodenough [3]

Viktor Frankl, a Viennese psychiatrist, has pioneered a new method of psychiatric treatment, logotherapy (meaning-therapy) claiming that the neurosis that many people experience is caused by a lack of meaning in their life. [4]

"Hello darkness, my old friend . . . " This song lyric by Simon and Garfunkel has almost a scriptural quality, and has struck a responsive chord in the millions who are haunted by its depth and meaning. Famous personalities travel to India to sit at the feet of bearded gurus in an attempt to put together the puzzle of life. Thousands of others flock to communes which daily grow in numbers across the United States. Steve Durkee, one of the founders of the Lama Foundation, a commune near Taos, New Mexico, attempts to give the interested observer some insight into the purpose of the commune with the following description:

> *The basic premise of the whole thing is that human beings have three bodies that need care and feeding . . . There is the physical body, which is most obvious; the mental body and the emotional or feeling body.*
>
> *We generally seem to be in a position where we exercise those bodies in different ways. A lot of university people get well exercised in the mental sphere, but not the physical.*
>
> *The hippie subculture is fantastically into the feeling body, but they're completely disorganized in their mental body.*
>
> *What we're working for is the development of the human personality through the harmonious growth of all three bodies.* [5]

[3] Ward H. Goodenough, *Human Purpose in Life,* **Zygon,** September 1966, p. 217.

[4] For a short and informative explanation of logotherapy see: Viktor E. Frankl, **Man's Search for Meaning** (New York: Washington Square Press, 1963).

[5] Steven V. Roberts, *Faithful Few Remain at Communes,* **The Minneapolis Tribune,** August 9, 1970.

"I'LL LET YOU KNOW THE MEANING OF LIFE WHEN I'M DARN GOOD AND READY"

Some turn to drugs. Others choose to live behind monastery walls for a lifetime of silence. Yet others, become master consumers of material goods and pleasures, in the footsteps of "Mr. Playboy", Hugh Hefner. What prompts people to style their lives in different fashions? What style suits you?

The Greek philosopher Socrates once said that the unexamined life is not worth living. Aristotle later claimed that we all adhere to a philosophy whether we are aware of it or not. Although some might advise you not to take life too seriously, and that excessive introspection may cause more problems than it presents answers for, man is by nature curious. He cannot be put off by suggestions to simply live life and not examine it. He constantly seeks answers to ultimate questions and attempts to discover the personal significance that answers to these questions may hold for him.

Every man needs a rudder that will give meaning and direction to his existence. The churches, the traditional sources of this guidance, seem to be losing their influence. Recent public opinion polls have revealed that religion, in the opinion of many of those polled, is losing its influence in American life.

If the churches, which for years have provided a ready-made philosophy for their membership, are losing influence, millions of people are going to have to use their own resources to construct a life philosophy. It is hoped that the following readings will provide a basis of comparison and a starting point for those who are interested in constructing such a philosophy.

Do not be misled. One cannot construct a life philosophy as the result of reading one book, or by participating in a stimulating discussion, or in some other singular fashion. Although an ancient eastern philosopher pointed out that the thousand mile journey begins with one step, the journey itself requires effort, patience and persistence.

In our technological age we are accustomed to traveling by jet and using instantaneous communications systems. We are unaccustomed to delays or even a substantial amount of effort in our traveling and communicating. This attitude, which many of us bring to most of our affairs, will be a hindrance in our quest for a life philosophy. There is no such thing as an instant life philosophy. Its development will take study, thought and time.

We must also overcome another handicap that our culture of today imposes on us. Too many are concerned with life style rather than substance. How many people take up the fad of the moment? How many people flit from book to movie to hobby, like a butterfly from flower to flower, and never become engrossed or committed to any one interest? We Americans have too little "staying power. " It is the style to taste lightly of everything and rarely does one investigate a new interest in depth. How many people read only the first chapters of books and spend their evenings switching the television dial from station to station? It is remarkable that so many Americans complain of boredom and a meaningless existence when no society has ever had such a wide variety of occupations, ideas, gadgets, books, churches, groups, etc., to capture their attention and give their lives meaning. The temptation today is to get "turned on" rather than involved in something.

Do not expect a burning bush or a voice from heaven to recommend a life philosophy. Consider the following readings with an open mind and a sense of curiosity. Investigate in depth those that interest you. But remember, a certain quality of mental self-discipline is necessary to really in-

6

vestigate another's life philosophy statement.[6] It is hoped that this collection of alternative life statements will strike a responsive chord within every reader, and lead him to a thoughtful examination of a philosophy that may suit him.

[6] Not all of the following readings can be considered complete life philosophy statements. Some present a formula or maxims to help in making a decision when faced with a complex moral issue. Others suggest explanations for the existence of the universe, and one reading, by Ann Landers, may be simply called advice.

DEVELOPING AN OPEN MIND

THE PARABLE OF THE CAVE
by Plato*

Plato, the greatest pupil of Socrates, was also the founder of one of the first colleges, the Academy. He lived in Athens from 427-347 B.C. The first reading is taken from **The Republic**, in which he uses Socrates as a spokesman to explore the nature of justice.

Before examining the alternatives in the following pages, you must first become aware of your tendency to prejudge (prejudice), to be biased, and to approach new ideas with a closed mind.

It has been said that man is a creature of habit. He is generally more comfortable when he can live his life accepting things with a minimum of questioning. He is usually satisfied with the political system, eating habits, economic practices, and

*From **The Great Dialogues of Plato,** translated by W.H.D. Rouse, edited by Eric H. Warmington & Philip G. Rouse. Copyright © 1956, 1961 by John Clive Graves Rouse. Reprinted by arrangement with The New American Library, Inc., New York, N.Y.

moral standards he inherited from his parents. He may even consider these systems the best of all possible systems and defend them vigorously. In short, he finds it easier to continue living in the manner to which he is accustomed. To change any of these systems would involve a great amount of effort and perhaps pain of one kind or another. Change is rarely easy. Revolution, an extreme form of change, usually involves bloodshed.

Because of man's predisposition to accept things as he finds them, and even consider them best, he is not always open to new suggestions. The following reading examines this tendency of man. Read it carefully to discover what lessons it can teach you. Hopefully, it will help you to approach the different life statements in this book with an open mind.

Consider these questions as you read:

1. Socrates suggests that we are all prisoners of some sort. What imprisons us?
2. Socrates also makes the point that it is often easier to live with falsehoods than with truth. What example does he use to illustrate this? Can you think of an example from your life experience?
3. How does Socrates show that ignorance or prejudice predisposes one to reject reality? Can you think of an example in contemporary society?

"Next, then," I said, *"take the following parable of education and ignorance as a picture of the condition of our nature. Imagine mankind as dwelling in an underground cave with a long entrance open to the light across the whole width of the cave; in this they have been from childhood, with necks and legs fettered, so they have to stay where they are. They cannot move their heads round because of the fetters, and they can only look forward, but light comes to them from fire burning behind them higher up at a distance. Between the fire and the prisoners is a road above their level, and along it imagine a low wall has been built, as puppet showmen have screens in front of their people over which they work their puppets."*

[See illustration on page 10]

9

"I see," he said.

"See, then, bearers carrying along this wall all sorts of articles which they hold projecting above the wall, statues of men and other living things,[1] made of stone or wood and all kinds of stuff, some of the bearers speaking and some silent, as you might expect."

"What a remarkable image," he said, "and what remarkable prisoners!"

"Just like ourselves," I said. "For, first of all, tell me this: What do you think such people would have seen of themselves and each other except their shadows, which the fire cast on the opposite wall of the cave?"

THE CAVE

[1] Including models of trees, etc.

10

"I don't see how they could see anything else," said he, "if they were compelled to keep their heads unmoving all their lives!"

"Very well, what of the things being carried along? Would not this be the same?"

"Of course it would."

"Suppose the prisoners were able to talk together, don't you think that when they named the shadows which they saw passing they would believe they were naming things?"[2]

"Necessarily."

"Then if their prison had an echo from the opposite wall, whenever one of the passing bearers uttered a sound, would they not suppose that the passing shadow must be making the sound? Don't you think so?"

"Indeed I do," he said.

"If so," said I, "such persons would certainly believe that there were no realities except those shadows of hand-made things."[3]

"So it must be," said he.

"Now consider," said I, "what their release would be like, and their cure from these fetters and their folly; let us imagine whether it might naturally be something like this. One might be released, and compelled suddenly to stand up and turn his neck round, and to walk and look towards the firelight; all this would hurt him, and he would be too much dazzled to see distinctly those things whose shadows he had seen before. What do you think he would say, if someone told him that what he saw before was foolery, but now he saw more rightly, being a bit nearer reality, and turned towards what was a little more real? What if he were shown each of the passing things, and compelled by questions to answer what each one was? Don't you think he would be puzzled, and believe what he saw before was more true than what was shown to him now?"

---

[2] Which they had never seen. They would say "tree" when it was only a shadow of the model of a tree.

[3] Shadows of artificial things, not even the shadow of a growing tree: another stage from reality.

"Far more," he said.

"Then suppose he were compelled to look towards the real light, it would hurt his eyes, and he would escape by turning them away to the things which he was able to look at, and these he would believe to be clearer than what was being shown to him."

"Just so," said he.

"Suppose, now," said I, *"that someone should drag him thence by force, up the rough ascent, the steep way up, and never stop until he could drag him out into the light of the sun, would he not be distressed and furious at being dragged; and when he came into the light, the brilliance would fill his eyes and he would not be able to see even one of the things now called real?"*[4]

"That he would not," said he, *"all of a sudden."*

"He would have to get used to it, surely, I think, if he is to see the things above. First he would most easily look at shadows, after that images of mankind and the rest in water, lastly the things themselves. After this he would find it easier to survey by night the heavens themselves and all that is in them, gazing at the light of the stars and moon, rather than by day the sun and the sun's light."

"Of course."

"Last of all, I suppose, the sun; he could look on the sun itself by itself in its own place, and see what it is like, not reflections of it in water or as it appears in some alien setting."

"Necessarily," said he.

"And only after all this he might reason about it, how this is he who provides seasons and years, and is set over all there is in the visible region, and he is in a manner the cause of all things which they saw."

"Yes, it is clear," said he, *"that after all that, he would come to this last."*

"Very good. Let him be reminded of his first habitation, and what was wisdom in that place, and of his fellow-prisoners there; don't you think he would bless himself for the change, and pity them?"

---

[4] To the next stage of knowledge: the real thing, not the artificial puppet.

"Yes, indeed."

"And if there were honours and praises among them and prizes for the one who saw the passing things most sharply and remembered best which of them used to come before and which after and which together, and from these was best able to prophesy accordingly what was going to come — do you believe he would set his desire on that, and envy those who were honoured men or potentates among them? Would he not feel as Homer says,[5] and heartily desire rather to be serf of some landless man on earth and to endure anything in the world, rather than to opine as they did and to live in that way?"

"Yes, indeed," said he, *"he would rather accept anything than live like that."*

"Then again," I said, *"just consider; if such a one should go down again and sit on his old seat, would he not get his eyes full of darkness coming in suddenly out of the sun?"*

"Very much so," said he.

"And if he should have to compete with those who had been always prisoners, by laying down the law about those shadows while he was blinking before his eyes were settled down — and it would take a good long time to get used to things — wouldn't they all laugh at him and say he had spoiled his eyesight by going up there, and it was not worthwhile so much as to try to go up? And would they not kill anyone who tried to release them and take them up, if they could somehow lay hands on him and kill him?"[6]

"That they would!" said he.

"Then we must apply this image, my dear Glaucon," said I, *"to all we have been saying. The world of our sight is like the habitation in prison, the firelight there to the sunlight here, the ascent and the view of the upper world is the rising of the soul into the world of mind; put it so and you will not be far from my own surmise, since that is what you want to hear; but God knows if it is really true. At least, what appears to me is, that in the world of known, last of all,[7] is the idea of the good, and with what toil to be seen!*

---

[5] **Odyssey** xi. 489.

[6] Plato probably alludes to the death of Socrates. See Apology, p. 444.

[7] The end of our search.

And seen, this must be inferred to be the cause of all right and beautiful things for all, which gives birth to light and the king of light in the world of sight, and, in the world of mind, herself the queen produces truth and reason; and she must be seen by one who is to act with reason publicly or privately."

UNDERSTANDING SYMBOLS

Many writers do not say exactly what they mean. They prefer to approach their subject in an indirect manner, often using symbols and parables to stimulate their readers to draw their own conclusions. Those who are familiar with the Gospels understand this technique. Jesus often told stories (parables) to make a point clear to his followers.

Plato uses this same technique in *"The Parable of the Cave."* He uses many symbols in the story so that the reader may come to a more penetrating understanding of the problem he is discussing.

Many writers use methods similar to those used by Jesus and Plato. If you wish to have a more intelligent understanding of your reading you must develop the skill of discovering the meaning writers intend in their use of parables and symbols. This exercise allows you to practice with symbols. The symbols below are used by Plato in the first reading. Reflect on their meaning, and discuss with your classmates the significance of each of them in the context of the parable and in terms of our contemporary society and in your own life experience.

Symbol	Plato's Intention	Significance in Contemporary Society
Cave	_____	_____
Fetters	_____	_____
Bearers	_____	_____
Things held up	_____	_____
Shadows	_____	_____
Naming of objects	_____	_____
Guide to the surface	_____	_____
Roadway	_____	_____
Sunlight	_____	_____

ALTERNATIVE 1

THE CHRISTIAN'S
COMMANDMENTS

from The Jerusalem Bible*

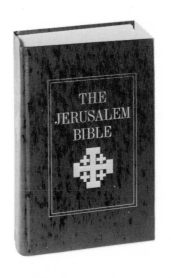

The **Jerusalem Bible** is an English translation of the famous French **Bible de Jerusalem** which was pieced together by experts from ancient Greek and Hebrew texts. It is a monumental achievement of scholarship, reflecting decades of research, study and translation.

*Excerpts from **The Jerusalem Bible,** copyright ©˙ 1966 by Darton, Longman and Todd, LTD. Doubleday & Company, Inc. Used by permission of the publisher.

> Eastern Orthodox Christians worship in ornate cathedrals while Quakers regard even a steeple as a desecration. St. Thomas finds no theological doctrine acceptable if it goes against reason while Tertullian cries *"I believe because it is absurd."* There are Christian mystics and Christians who denounce mysticism as beginning in *"mist,"* centering in *I,"* and ending in *"scism."* Albertus Magnus finds religious meaning in cracking the hard nut of a theological argument, St. Francis in preaching to birds and flowers. There are Christian Holy Rollers and Christian Unitarians."

Huston Smith, **The Religions of Man** (New York: Harper & Row, 1958), p. 3.

It is perhaps an ambitious undertaking to present a Christian statement that could be considered representative of the many millions of Christians, alive and dead, who have been influenced by the teachings of Jesus, for the message of Jesus has been interpreted differently by those who call themselves his followers. In spite of this difficulty, probably all Christians would admit that the following words from the Bible form the core of their belief structures.

These questions may help your understanding of the reading:

1. How does the standard of behavior in the New Testament differ from the commandments laid down in the Old Testament?
2. What one commandment can be said to sum up all the others?

OLD TESTAMENT
BOOK OF DEUTERONOMY
5:1-22

Moses called the whole of Israel together and said to them:

The Ten Commandments

'Listen, Israel, to the laws and customs that I proclaim in your hearing today. Learn them and take care to observe them.

18

'Yahweh our God made a covenant with us at Horeb. It was not with our fathers that Yahweh made this covenant, but with us, with us who are here, all living today. On the mountain, from the heart of the fire, Yahweh spoke to you face to face, and I stood all the time between Yahweh and yourselves to tell you of Yahweh's words, for you were afraid of the fire and had not gone up the mountain. He said :

"I am Yahweh your God who brought you out of the land of Egypt, out of the house of slavery.

"You shall have no gods except me.

"You shall not make yourself a carved image or any likeness of anything in heaven above or on earth beneath or in the waters under the earth; you shall not bow down to them or serve them. For I, Yahweh your God, am a jealous God and I punish the fathers' fault in the sons, the grandsons and the great-grandsons of those who hate me; but I show kindness to thousands, to those who love me and keep my commandments.

"You shall not utter the name of Yahweh your God to misuse it, for Yahweh will not leave unpunished the man who utters his name to misuse it.

"Observe the sabbath day and keep it holy, as Yahweh your God has commanded you. For six days you shall labour and do all your work, but the seventh day is a sabbath for Yahweh your God. You shall do no work that day, neither you nor your son nor your daughter nor your servants, men or women, nor your ox nor your donkey nor any of your animals, nor the stranger who lives with you. Thus your servant, man or woman, shall rest as you do. Remember that you were a servant in the land of Egypt, and that Yahweh your God brought you out from there with mighty hand and outstretched arm; because of this, Yahweh your God has commanded you to keep the sabbath day.

"Honour your father and your mother, as Yahweh your God has commanded you, so that you may have long life and may prosper in the land that Yahweh your God gives to you.

"You shall not kill.

"You shall not commit adultery.

"You shall not steal.

"You shall not bear false witness against your neighbour.

"You shall not covet your neighbour's wife, you shall not set your heart on his house, his field, his servant — man or woman — his ox, his donkey or anything that is his."

'These are the words Yahweh spoke to you when you were all assembled on the mountain. With a great voice he spoke to you from the heart of the fire, in cloud and thick darkness. He added nothing, but wrote them on two tablets of stone which he gave to me.'

NEW TESTAMENT
GOSPEL ACCORDING TO ST. MATTHEW
5:17-48

The fulfilment of the Law

'Do not imagine that I have come to abolish the Law or the Prophets. I have come not to abolish but to complete them. I tell you solemnly, till heaven and earth disappear, not one dot, not one little stroke, shall disappear from the Law until its purpose is achieved. Therefore, the man who infringes even one of the least of these commandments and teaches others to do the same will be considered the least in the kingdom of heaven; but the man who keeps them and teaches them will be considered great in the kingdom of heaven.

The new standard higher than the old

'For I tell you, if your virtue goes no deeper than that of the scribes and Pharisees, you will never get into the kingdom of heaven.

'You have learnt how it was said to our ancestors: You must not kill; and if anyone does kill he must answer for it before the court. But I say this to you: anyone who is angry with his brother will answer for it before the court; if a man calls his brother "Fool" he will answer for it before the Sanhedrin; and if a man calls him "Renegade" he will answer for it in hell fire. So then, if you are bringing your offering to the altar and there remember that your brother has something against you, leave your offering there before the altar, go and be reconciled with your brother first, and then come back and present your offering. Come to terms with your opponent in good time while you are still on the way to the court with him, or he may hand you over to the *judge and the judge to the officer, and you will be thrown into prison. I tell you solemnly, you will not get out till you have paid the last penny.*

'You have learnt how it was said: *You must not commit* adultery. *But I say this to you: if a man looks at a woman lustfully, he has already committed adultery with her in his heart. If your right eye should cause you to sin, tear it out and throw it away; for it will do you less harm to lose one part of you than to have your whole body thrown into hell. And if your right hand should cause you to sin, cut it off and throw it away; for it will do you less harm to lose one part of you than to have your whole body go to hell.*

'*It has also been said:* Anyone who divorces his wife must give her a writ of dismissal. *But I say this to you: everyone who divorces his wife, except for the case of fornication, makes her an adulteress; and anyone who marries a divorced woman commits adultery.*

'*Again, you have learnt how it was said to our ancestors:* You must not break your oath, but must fulfil your oaths to the Lord. *But I say this to you: do not swear at all, either by heaven, since that is God's throne; or by* the earth, *since that is* his footstool; *or by Jerusalem, since that is* the city of the great king. *Do not swear by your own head either, since you cannot turn a single hair white or black. All you need say is "Yes" if you mean yes, "No" if you mean no; anything more than this comes from the evil one.*

'You have learnt how it was said: Eye for eye and tooth for tooth. *But I say this to you: offer the wicked man no resistance. On the contrary, if anyone hits you on the right cheek, offer him the other as well; if a man takes you to law and would have your tunic, let him have your cloak as well. And if anyone orders you to go one mile, go two miles with him. Give to anyone who asks, and if anyone wants to borrow, do not turn away.*

'You have learnt how it was said: You must love your neighbour and hate your enemy. *But I say this to you: love your enemies and pray for those who persecute you; in this way you will be sons of your Father in heaven, for he causes his sun to rise on bad men as well as good, and his rain to fall on honest and dishonest men alike. For if you love those who love you, what right have you to claim any credit? Even the tax collectors do as much, do they not? And if you save your greetings for your brothers, are you doing anything exceptional? Even the pagans do as much, do they not? You must therefore be perfect just as your heavenly Father is perfect.'*

LETTER TO THE ROMANS
13:9-10

All the commandments: You shall not commit adultery, you shall not kill, you shall not steal, you shall not covet, *and so on, are summed up in this single command:* You must love your neighbour as yourself. *Love is the one thing that cannot hurt your neighbour; that is why it is the answer to every one of the commandments.*

ALTERNATIVE 2

ADVICE FOR A PRINCE

by Niccolo Machiavelli*

> **The Prince**, which was intended as practical advice to the Medici princes to aid them in governing, was published in 1532, five years after the death of Machiavelli. The reading below suggests that decisions be made solely on the basis of their practical consequences with no consideration given to ethical principles.

As you read consider the following questions:

1. Under what circumstances does Machiavelli suggest that a ruler not keep faith?
2. What does Machiavelli mean when he says *"the end justifies the means"*?
3. What kind of a personal life philosophy do you think Machiavelli would recommend for you in our contemporary society?

---

*From **The Prince** by Niccolo Machiavelli, translated by Luigi Ricci, revised by E R P Vincent and published by Oxford University Press, pp. 92-94.

How laudable it is for a prince to keep good faith and live with integrity, and not with astuteness, every one knows. Still the experience of our times shows those princes to have done great things who have had little regard for good faith, and have been able by astuteness to confuse men's brains, and who have ultimately overcome those who have made loyalty their foundation.

You must know, then, that there are two methods of fighting, the one by law, the other by force: the first method is that of men, the second of beasts; but as the first method is often insufficient, one must have recourse to the second. It is therefore necessary for a prince to know well how to use both the beast and the man. This was covertly taught to rulers by ancient writers, who relate how Achilles and many others of those ancient princes were given to Chiron the centaur to be brought up and educated under his discipline. The parable of this semi-animal, semi-human teacher is meant to indicate that a prince must know how to use both natures, and that the one without the other is not durable.

> **A prudent ruler ought not to keep faith when by so doing it would be against his interest, and when the reasons which make him bind himself no longer exist. If men were all good, this precept would not be a good one; but as they are bad, and would not observe their faith with you, so you are not bound to keep faith with them.**

A prince being thus obliged to know well how to act as a beast must imitate the fox and the lion, for the lion cannot protect himself from traps, and the fox cannot defend himself from wolves. One must therefore be a fox to recognize traps, and a lion to frighten wolves. Those that wish to be only lions do not understand this. Therefore, a prudent ruler ought not to keep faith when by so doing it would be against his interest, and when the reasons which made him bind himself no longer exist. If men were all good, this precept would not be a good one; but as they are bad, and would not observe their faith with you, so you are not bound to keep faith with them. Nor have legitimate grounds ever failed a prince who wished to show colourable excuse for the non-fulfilment of his promise. Of this one could furnish an infinite number of modern examples, and show how many times peace has been broken, and how many promises rendered worthless, by the faithlessness of princes, and those that have been best able to imitate the fox have succeeded best. But it is necessary to be able to disguise this character well, and to be a great feigner and dissembler; and men are so simple and so ready to obey present necessities, that one who deceives will always find those who allow themselves to be deceived.

I will only mention one modern instance. Alexander VI did nothing else but deceive men, he thought of nothing else, and found the occasion for it; no man was ever more able to give assurances, or affirmed things with stronger oaths, and no man observed them less; however, he always succeeded in his deceptions, as he well knew this aspect of things.

It is not, therefore, necessary for a prince to have all the above-named qualities, but it is very necessary to seem to have them. I would even be bold to say that to possess them and always to observe them is dangerous, but to appear to possess them is useful. Thus it is well to seem merciful, faithful, humane, sincere, religious, and also to be so; but you must have the mind so disposed that when it is needful to be otherwise you may be able to change to the opposite qualities. And it must be understood that a prince, and especially a new prince, cannot observe all those things which are considered good in men, being often obliged, in order to maintain the state, to act against faith, against charity, against humanity, and against religion. And, therefore, he must have a mind disposed to adapt itself according to the wind, and as the variations of fortune dictate, and, as I said before, not deviate from what is good, if possible, but be able to do evil if constrained.

A prince must take great care that nothing goes out of his mouth which is not full of the above-named five qualities, and, to see and hear him, he should seem to be all mercy, faith, integrity, humanity, and religion. And nothing is more necessary than to seem to have this last quality, for men in general judge more by the eyes than by the hands, for every one can see, but very few have to feel. Everybody sees what you appear to be, few feel what you are, and those few will not dare to oppose themselves to the many, who have the majesty of the state to defend them; and in the actions of men, and especially of princes, from which there is no appeal, the end justifies the means. Let a prince therefore aim at conquering and maintaining the state, and the means will always be judged honourable and praised by every one, for the vulgar is always taken by appearances and the issue of the event; and the world consists only of the vulgar, and the few who are not vulgar are isolated when the many have a rallying point in the prince. A certain prince of the present time, whom it is well not to name, never does anything but preach peace and good faith, but he is really a great enemy to both, and either of them, had he observed them, would have lost him state or reputation on many occasions.

DETERMINING VALUES

This exercise will give you an opportunity to see what values you consider important. It will also enable you to decide with your classmates the values the class considers most important.

Part I

Instructions

Step 1. The class should break into groups of four to six students.

Step 2. Working individually, within each group, each student should rank the values on page 28, assigning the number (1) to the value considered most important, the number (2) to the second most important value, and so on, until all the values have been ranked.

Step 3. Each student should compare his ranking with others in the group, giving the reasons for his ranking.

Part II

Instructions

Working either in small groups of four to six students or all together, the class should examine the two pictures on page 29. Discuss the following questions relating to the two pictures.

1. What specific values can you identify and associate with the pictures?
2. Which of these values do you identify most closely with? Which do you identify least closely with?

VALUES TO BE RANKED

_____ Material comfort

_____ Inner peace

_____ Commitment to a cause

_____ An adverterous lifestyle

_____ Friendship

_____ Financial security

_____ Self-respect

_____ Courage

_____ Popularity or fame

_____ Freedom

_____ Service to others

_____ Love

BILLY GRAHAM'S PHILOSOPHY

by Billy Graham*

Reverend Billy Graham, the founder of the Billy Graham Evangelistic Association, has preached the message of Jesus to more people than any other individual in history. His counsel has been sought by the past four presidents of the United States, and for the last ten years he has ranked among the ten most admired men in the world. The reading that follows is an address he delivered at a Harvard Law Forum public meeting and at the University of Chicago in 1962.

Reflect on the following questions while you read:

1. What causes man's weakness, in the opinion of the Reverend Graham?
2. Why does the Reverend Graham place so much emphasis on the cross?
3. What roles do reason and faith play in understanding life?
4. In what sense does the Reverend Graham advocate narrowmindedness? Do you agree?

THE GATEWAY TO TRUTH

An outstanding mathematician visited me recently and said, *"If anyone had told me five years ago that I would be coming to see you, I would have laughed. But I am at the end of myself, and I am going to commit suicide unless I find an answer to what I am facing."*

His problems were neither domestic nor financial nor vocational; they were problems of emptiness that he could not explain. He belonged to the world of the misfits, the world of lost people. Ours is an age of philosophical uncertainty, and we no longer know what we believe. We stand uncommitted. I ask students everywhere I go, *"What is controlling you?"*

> **Man does need commitment to a call, to a goal, to a flag. Does it work when a man comes, repenting of his sins, to receive Christ by faith? I can only tell you that it worked in my own life. Something did happen to me. I didn't become perfect, but the direction of my life was changed.**

Eugene O'Neill in *"Long Day's Journey Into Night"* expresses a philosophical attitude we find so prevalent today. *"Life's only meaning,"* he says, *"is death, so face it with courage and even with love of the inevitable. Death becomes a blanket on a cold night."* Jean-Paul Sartre, the French existentialist, has said, *"There is no exit from the human dilemma."*

When we seek to get to the root of our problems, we discover that many writers and thinkers are saying that the problem is man himself. Dr. J.S. Whale asked the undergraduates at Cambridge University, *"What is man? Where did he come from? Why is he here? Where is he going? What is the purpose and destiny of the human race?"* Dr. John A. Mackay told the students at Princeton, *"The anthropological problem is the crucial problem of our generation."*

SHADOW CAST BY IMMATURITY?

There are psychologists and psychiatrists who are beginning to admit that something is basically wrong with human nature. Some say it is a shadow cast by man's immaturity; others describe it as a deficiency determined by heredity and environment; still others call it a constitutional weakness. **It is time to ask what the Bible has to say** — this old book that some have dismissed by saying it is irrelevant in the twentieth century.

The Bible calls the trouble inside of man by an ugly word. We don't like this old word — we prefer the new jargon — but I am going to use the old word. The Bible calls it sin. It tells us that man's soul has a disease. You ask me where sin comes from and I cannot tell you; I do not know. The Bible speaks of it as *"the mystery of iniquity."* God has not seen fit to reveal to us the origin of this tragic disease that has gripped the entire human race.

Suppose I visit the Auca Indians in Ecuador, as I did a few years ago. There I find people living in the Stone Age. I see them lying, cheating, hating, killing. War has almost completely annihilated the various tribes of the Auca Indians. I say to myself, *"What these people need is education, economic security, better food, better clothes."* It is true that they need them all. But when I come to New York, and Paris, and London, and Moscow, what do I find? People who have all of these advantages, and who are still lying, hating, cheating and killing. The most devastating wars of history have been fought by the so-called civilized countries.

A SCHWEITZER AND AN EICHMANN

How can a country like Germany produce in one generation an Albert Schweitzer and an Adolf Eichmann? Somethng is basically wrong. How could Joseph Goebbels, who secured his doctor's degree at Heidelberg University, become the man he was?

Many words in the Bible are translated *"sin."* A transgression of the law is sin. To miss the mark is sin. Isaiah the prophet declared, *"Your iniquities have separated between you and your God, and your sins have hid his face from you, that he will not hear"* (Isaiah 59:2). Jesus Christ charged the Pharisees with leaving undone the things they ought to have done, and He said, *"Whosoever committeth sin is the servant of sin"* (John 8:34). This thing affects the mind, it affects the conscience. It affects the will, it causes conflict with others. Sin controls the ego, which is self. Christ said we are to love God first and self last, but sin has reversed that.

Archbishop William Temple once said, *"Sin makes 'me' the center of the world."* We become selfish as individuals, as a nation, as a society. Sin, the Bible says, eventually brings judgment — *"The wages of sin is death."* It creates its own hell on this earth as well as in the life to come. For you see, you and I were made for God, and without God there is always an emptiness and restlessness. We quest and search and try to find fulfillment in life, but we never quite attain it.

WHEN GOD TOOK THE INITIATIVE

I cannot prove to you the existence of God. I see evidences of God, and something down inside me tells me that there must be a God. Furthermore, I have never found a tribe that didn't believe in a god of some sort. If we don't have a God we make a god; anything that is higher than ourselves becomes a god. But the Bible indicates not only that there is a God, but that He took the initiative; that the mighty God of all the universe has spoken and has revealed Himself in a person, and that that person is Jesus Christ.

Why does the church put so much emphasis on the Cross? Because the Cross is the heart of Christianity. On that Cross in some mysterious way Christ died for us. God took our sins, our breaking of the law that caused us to deserve death and judgment, and He laid our sins on Christ. As the Scripture says, He was made sin for us (2 Corinthians 5:21).

When I was a student I had to face Christ. Who was He? He had made the astounding claim, *"I am the way, the truth, and the life; no man cometh unto the Father but by me."* I wrestled with the inescapable fact that either Jesus Christ was who He claimed to be, or He was the biggest liar, fraud and charlatan in history. Which was it? Buddha said toward the end of his life, *"I am still searching for the truth."* But here was a man who appeared and said, *"I am the embodiment of all truth. All truth is centered in me."*

One day by a simple act of faith I decided to take Jesus Christ at His word. I could not come by way of the intellect alone; no one can. That does not mean that we reject reason. God has given us minds and the ability to reason

33

wherever reason is appropriate, but the final and decisive step is taken by faith. I came by faith.

A few years ago I was invited to lunch by the head of the department of psychology at an eastern university. He remarked to me, *"We have come to believe that man is so constituted psychologically that he needs converting, especially in later adolescence. In order to find fulfillment, young people need converting."* In the New York *Times* a professional psychiatrist wrote, *"Unless the church gets back to converting the people, we psychiatrists are going to have to do it."*

IT HAS WORKED IN MY LIFE

What Jesus Christ said about conversion was not only theologically true, it was also psychologically sound. Man does need commitment to a call, to a goal, to a flag. Does it work when a man comes, repenting of his sins, to receive Christ by faith? I can only tell you that it worked in my own life. Something did happen to me. I didn't become perfect, but the direction of my life was changed.

I was reared on a farm in North Carolina, and did not have the best of education. During the depression period my parents were unable to give me the advantages that youth has today. I grew up in a Christian home, but by the time I was 15, I was in full revolt against all religion — against God, the Bible, the church. To make a long story short, one day I decided to commit my life to Jesus Christ. Not to be a clergyman but, in whatever I was to be, to seek the Kingdom of God first.

As a result, I found a new dimension to life. I found a new capacity to love that I had never known before. Just in the matter of race, my attitude toward people of other backgrounds changed remarkably. All of our difficulties are not solved the moment we are converted to Christ, but conversion does mean that we can approach our problems with a new attitude and in a new strength.

MEN'S HEARTS ARE FASHIONED ALIKE

I was a poor student until that time, but immediately my grades picked up. I am not suggesting that you should come to Christ in order to get better grades, but I am telling you that the life in Christ works. I have seen it work all over the world. I have seen those converted whom I might classify as intellectuals; but they have to come as children. We say to our children, *"Act like grown-ups,"* but Jesus said to the grown-ups, *"Be like children."* You are not to come to the Cross as a doctor of philosophy, or as a doctor of law, but simply as a human being; and your life can be changed.

You ask, *"Does it take with everybody?"* Yes, with everyone who is willing to believe. I don't find that anyone is excluded. I have become confirmed in my belief that the Bible is right in saying that God has fashioned the hearts of men alike. We are not together in today's world linguistically, culturally or racially. We are divided. We have become a neighborhood without being a brotherhood. Yet there is one area in which I am convinced we are all alike —

the spiritual dimension. I believe the hearts of all of us are the same. Our deep needs are identical the world over, for they come from within. Our need is God.

Probably it sounds a bit intolerant and narrow to you for an evangelist to go around the planet preaching the Cross — and you are right; for Jesus said that the gate to the Kingdom of Heaven is narrow. But we are narrow also in mathematics and in chemistry. If we weren't narrow in chemistry we would be blowing the place up. We have to be narrow. I am glad that pilots are not so broadminded that they come into an airport any way they want.

Why then should we not be narrow when it comes to moral laws and spiritual dimensions? I believe that Christ is different; that He is unique. I believe that He is the Son of the living God and that He did change my life.

HOW WILL IT ALL END?

Many intellectuals are asking where history is going; they are speculating on what the end will be. I believe that Christ's prayer, *"Thy kingdom come. Thy will be done in earth, as it is in heaven"* — the prayer that you and I often pray — is going to be answered. And when the human race stands at the edge of the abyss, ready to blow itself apart, I believe God will intervene in history again. I don't believe any world leader will write the last chapter of history. I believe God will write it. I believe that the future kingdom is going to be the Kingdom of God, that there is a destiny for the human race far beyond anything we can dream. But it will be God's kingdom and will come in God's way.

Meanwhile He is calling people from all walks of life to follow His Son, Jesus Christ. I know that those who respond are a minority, but Christ used a minority while He was on earth. When He died on the Cross only 120 of His followers could be mustered. Yet within a short time, according to the testimony of the people of that day, they had *"turned the world upside down."*

In Moscow some years ago I saw 50,000 students gathered in Red Square, stamping their feet and chanting, *"We're going to change the world. We're going to change the world!"* I thought to myself, what if we could get students in the United States and all around the world, including the Soviet Union and China, to march under the banner of Christ? Why couldn't we be a dedicated minority, committed to Jesus Christ, with love in our hearts and with

His flag to follow? I am asking this of students everywhere I go.

I believe that if we can light a few torches here and there on campuses on every continent, we might have a spiritual revolution that would really change the world. Here, in this dimension, lies our hope for humanity. We can argue and debate the old philosophical problems from now on, and die without committing ourselves to anything; or we can march in the army of Jesus Christ. Which will it be?

THE NEW MORALITY

by Joseph Fletcher*

Joseph Fletcher, distin-
guished educator and
theologian, is Professor of
Medical Ethics at the University of Virginia School of
Medicine.

As you read try to answer the following questions:

1. According to Fletcher there are three ways to make a
    moral decision. What are they and how do they differ?
2. What is the one commandment that the Christian situa-
    tionalist observes?
3. What distinction does the situationalist make between
    principles and rules?

*From **Situation Ethics**, by Joseph Fletcher. Copyright © MCMLXVI,
by W.L. Jenkins, The Westminster Press. Used by permission.

There are at bottom only three alternative routes or approaches to follow in making moral· decisions. They are: (1) the legalistic; (2) the antinomian, the opposite extreme — i.e., a lawless or unprincipled approach; and (3) the situational. All three have played their part in the history of Western morals, legalism being by far the most common and persistent. Just as legalism triumphed among the Jews after the exile, so, in spite of Jesus' and Paul's revolt against it, it has managed to dominate Christianity constantly from very early days. As we shall be seeing, in many real-life situations legalism demonstrates what Henry Miller, in a shrewd phrase, calls *"the immorality of morality."*[1] . . .

APPROACHES TO DECISION-MAKING

1. LEGALISM

With this approach one enters into every decision-making situation encumbered with a whole apparatus of prefabricated rules and regulations. Not just the spirit but the letter of the law reigns. Its principles, codified in rules, are not merely guidelines or maxims to illuminate the situation; they are *directives* to be followed. Solutions are preset, and you can *"look them up"* in a book — a Bible or a confessor's manual.

Judaism, Catholicism, Protestantism — all major Western religious traditions have been legalistic. In morals as in doctrine they have kept to a spelled-out, *"systematic"* orthodoxy. . . .

2. ANTINOMIANISM

Over against legalism, as a sort of polar opposite, we can put antinomianism. This is the approach with which one enters into the decision-making situation armed with no principles or maxims whatsoever, to say nothing of *rules.* In every *"existential moment"* or *"unique"* situation, it declares, one must rely upon the situation of itself, *there and then*, to provide its ethical solution. . . .

---

[1] **Stand Still Like the Hummingbird** (New Directions, 1962), pp. 92-96.

3. SITUATIONISM

A third approach, in between legalism and antinomian unprincipledness, is situation ethics. (To jump from one polarity to the other would be only to go from the frying pan to the fire.) The situationist enters into every decision-making situation fully armed with the ethical maxims of his community and its heritage, and he treats them with respect as illuminators of his problems. Just the same he is prepared in any situation to compromise them or set them aside *in the situation* if love seems better served by doing so.

Christian situation ethics has only one norm or principle or law (call it what you will) that is binding and unexceptionable, always good and right regardless of the circumstances. That is "love" — the agape of the summary commandment to love God and the neighbor.

Situation ethics goes part of the way with natural law, by accepting reason as the instrument of moral judgment, while rejecting the notion that the good is *"given"* in the nature of things, objectively. It goes part of the way with Scriptural law by accepting revelation as the source of the norm while rejecting all *"revealed"* norms or laws but the one command — to love God in the neighbor. The situationist follows a moral law or violates it according to love's need. For example, *"almsgiving is a good thing if . . ."* The situationist never says, *"Almsgiving is a good thing. Period!"* His decisions are hypothetical, not categorical. Only the commandment to love is categorically good. *"Owe no one anything, except to love one another."* (Rom. 13:8.) If help to an indigent only pauperizes and degrades him, the situationist refuses a handout and finds some other way. He makes no law out of Jesus' *"Give to every one who begs from you."* . . .

Christian situation ethics has only one norm or principle or law (call it what you will) that is binding and unexceptionable, always good and right regardless of the circumstances. That is *"love"* — the *agape* of the summary commandment to love God and the neighbor.[22] Everything else without exception, all laws and rules and principles and ideals and norms, are only *contingent*, only valid *if they happen* to serve love in any situation. Christian situation ethics is not a system or program of living according to a code, but an effort to relate love to a world of relativities through a casuistry obedient to love. It is the strategy of love. This strategy denies that there are, as Sophocles thought, any unwritten immutable laws of heaven, agreeing with Bultmann that all such notions are idolatrous and a demonic pretension.[23] . . .

PRINCIPLES, YES, BUT NOT RULES

It is necessary to insist that situation ethics is willing to make full and respectful use of principles, to be treated as maxims but not as laws or precepts. We might call it *"principled relativism."* To repeat the term used above, principles of maxims or general rules are *illuminators.* But they are not *directors.* The classic rule of moral theology has been to follow laws but do it *as much as possible* according to love and according to reason (*secundum caritatem et secundum rationem*). Situation ethics, on the other hand, calls upon us to keep law in a subservient place, so that *only* love and reason really count when the chips are down! . . .

ABORTION: A SITUATION

In 1962 a patient in a state mental hospital raped a fellow patient, an unmarried girl ill with a radical schizophrenic psychosis. The victim's father, learning what had happened, charged the hospital with culpable negligence and requested that an abortion to end the unwanted pregnancy be performed at once, in an early stage of the embryo. The staff and administrators of the hospital refused to do so, on the ground that the criminal law forbids all abortion except *"therapeutic"* ones when the mother's life is at stake — because the *moral* law, it is supposed, holds that any interference with an embryo after fertilization is murder, i.e., the taking of an innocent human being's life.

[22] Matt. 5:43-48 and ch. 22:34-40; Luke 6:27-28; 10:25-28 and vs. 29-37; Mark 12:28-34; Gal. 5:14; Rom. 13:8-10; etc.

[23] Rudolf Bultmann, **Essays Philosophical and Theological** (The Macmillan Company, 1955), pp. 22, 154.

Let's relate the three ethical approaches to this situation. The rape has occurred and the decisional question is: May we rightly (licitly) terminate this pregnancy, begun in an act of force and violence by a mentally unbalanced rapist upon a frightened, mentally sick girl? Mother and embryo are apparently healthy on all the usual counts.

The legalists would say *NO*. Their position is that killing is absolutely wrong, inherently evil. It is permissible only as self-defense and in military service, which is held to be presumptive self-defense or justifiable homicide. If the mother's life is threatened, abortion is therefore justified, but for no other reasons. (Many doctors take an elastic view of *"life"* and thereby justify abortions to save a patient's *mental* life as well as physical.) Even in cases where they justify it, it is only excused — it is still held to be inherently evil. Many Protestants hold this view, and some humanists.

Catholic moral theology goes far beyond even the rigid legalism of the criminal law, absolutizing their prohibition of abortion *absolutely*, by denying all exceptions and calling even therapeutic abortion wrong. (They allow killing in self-defense against malicious, i.e., deliberate, aggressors but not in self-defense against innocent, i.e., unintentional aggressors.) Thus if it is a tragic choice of the mother's life or the baby's, as can happen in rare cases, neither can be saved.

To this ethical nightmare legalism replies: *"It is here that the Church appears merciless, but she is not. It is her logic which is merciless; and she promises that if the logic is followed the woman will receive a reward far greater than a number of years of life."*[40] Inexplicably, shockingly, Dietrich Bonhoeffer says the same thing: *"The life of the mother is in the hand of God, but the life of the child is arbitrarily extinguished. The question whether the life of the mother or the life of the child is of greater value can hardly be a matter for a human decision."*[41]

The antinomians — but who can predict what *they* would say? Their ethic is by its nature and definition outside the reach of even generalities. We can only guess, not unreasonably, that if the antinomian lives by a love norm, he will be apt to favor abortion in this case.

The situationists, if their norm is the Christian commandment to love the neighbor, would almost certainly, *in this case*, favor abortion and support the girl's father's request. (Many purely humanistic decision makers are of the same mind about abortion following rape, and after incest, too.) They would in all likelihood favor abortion for the sake of the patient's physical and mental health, not only if it were needed to save her life. It is even likely they would favor abortion for the sake of the victim's self-respect or reputation or happiness or simply on the ground that *no unwanted and unintended* baby should ever be born.

---

[40] Alan Keenan, O.F.M., and John Ryan, M.D., **Marriage: A Medical and Sacramental Study** (Sheed & Ward, Inc., 1955), p. 53.

[41] **Ethics,** p. 131n.

They would, one hopes, reason that it is *not* killing because there is no person or human life in an embryo at an early stage of pregnancy (Aristotle and St. Thomas held that opinion), or even if it *were* killing, it would not be murder because it is self-defense against, in this case, not one but *two* aggressors. First there is the rapist, who being insane was morally and legally innocent, and then there is the *"innocent"* embryo which is continuing the ravisher's original aggression! Even self-defense legalism would have allowed the girl to kill her attacker, no matter that he was innocent in the forum of conscience because of his madness. The embryo is no more innocent, no less an aggressor or unwelcome invader! Is not the most loving thing possible (the right thing) in this case a responsible decision to terminate the pregnancy?

What think ye?

GUIDELINES FOR TEACHING MORAL VALUES

A large part of an individual's life philosophy is determined for him by the values he is taught to believe and practice by his parents and teachers. Examine the following arguments that are often used in instilling value judgements in young people. Decide, with your classmates, the strengths and weaknesses of each argument, and then construct your own set of guidelines, the approach you would use in leading your children to a value structure to guide their lives by.

Argument #1: Children are not old enough or experienced enough or wise enough to choose values for themselves. We are responsible for starting them off on the right track. We have to drill values into children now; later they will learn to value for themselves.

Argument #2: It takes too much time to help children figure out their own values. It's faster and simpler to merely show them the best way.

Argument #3: Think of the problems that will develop from wrong choices! Time wasted, unnecessary hurt and pain, and perhaps even irreparable human damage. Besides, how can adults contain themselves when they see children going astray? What, after all, are adults for if they do not point the way to wisdom and righteousness?

Argument #4: Look, what can I do? Everyone else tries to give values to children. My children will think I'm crazy if I do otherwise, and certainly other adults will look at me and wonder at my laxness.*

*These four arguments are taken from the source: Louis E. Raths, Merrill Harmin and Sidney B. Simon, **Values and Teaching: Working With Values in the Classroom** (Columbus, Ohio: Charles E. Merrill Books, 1966), pp. 41-42. This is a helpful book for those who are interested in the problem of values in the classroom.

Your Guidelines:

_____

_____

_____

_____

_____

AN ATHEIST'S VALUES

by Richard Robinson*

Richard Robinson was born in Watton, Norfolk, England, in 1902. He was educated at Oxford University and taught philosophy at Cornell University from 1928 to 1946. In 1946 he returned to Oxford where he has since resided. His main publications are **Plato's Earlier Dialectic, Definition**, and **An Atheist's Values**.

Bring the following questions to your reading:

1. Why does Mr. Robinson claim that man is basically insecure?
2. How does this reading suggest man react to the problem of his existence?
3. Why does Mr. Robinson suggest that the atheist's conception of man is nobler than the theist's?
4. Why does this contributor suggest that we love one another?
5. Why does Mr. Robinson disapprove of religious ceremonies?

*Richard Robinson, **An Atheist's Values** (New York: Oxford University Press, 1964), pp. 155-57. Reprinted with permission from the Claredon Press, Oxford.

The human situation is this.

Each one of us dies. He ceases to pulse or breathe or move or think. He decays and loses his identity. His mind or soul or spirit ends with the ending of his body, because it is entirely dependent on his body.

The human species too will die one day, like all species of life. One day there will be no more men. This is not quite so probable as that each individual man will die; but it is overwhelmingly probable all the same. It seems very

> I do not believe there is a god, or any gods, personal or in nature, or manifesting himself, herself, or itself in any way. I do not believe there is such a thing as heaven, or hell, or perdition, or purgatory, or any other stages in between. I do not believe there is any life after death. I do not believe in miracles.
>
> I do not believe in angels. I do not believe in prophets and I do not accept any holy book of any kind, be it the Bible, the Koran, the Torah, the Veda, the Upanishads, or anything else in any age in the history of man.
>
> I do not believe in saviors and this includes any so-called saviors from Moses to Jesus Christ, or Mohammed, or his daughter Fatima, or Buddha, or the popes or any oracles, self-appointed or appointed by other persons.
>
> I do not believe in the efficacy of prayers said by myself, or a priest, a rabbi or a minister.
>
> I believe that, as adults, we must face the fact that this is silly. These ancient ideas are silly and we no longer need to cling to them. Some of these beliefs are an insult to you and to me. They are an insult to our intelligence, to our common sense, and to our own experience which we have gained from living.

Madalyn Murray O'Hair in **What On Earth Is An Atheist!**

unlikely that we could keep the race going for ever by hopping from planet to planet as each in turn cooled down. Only in times of extraordinary prosperity like the present could we ever travel to another planet at all.

We are permanently insecure. We are permanently in danger of loss, damage, misery, and death.

Our insecurity is due partly to our ignorance. There is a vast amount that we do not know, and some of it is very relevant to our survival and happiness. It is not just one important thing and live secure ever after. That one important thing would then deserve to be called 'the secret of the universe'. But there is no one secret of the universe. On the contrary, there are inexhaustibly many things about the universe that we need to know but do not know. There is no possibility of 'making sense of the universe', if that means discovering one truth about it which explains everything else about it and also explains itself. Our ignorance grows progressively less, at least during periods of enormous prosperity like the present time; but it cannot disappear, and must always leave us liable to unforeseen disasters.

The main cause of our insecurity is the limitedness of our power. What happens to us depends largely on forces we cannot always control. This will remain so throughout the life of our species, although our power will probably greatly increase.

There is no god to make up for the limitations of our power, to rescue us whenever the forces affecting us get beyond our control, or provide us hereafter with an incorruptible haven of absolute security. We have no superhuman father who is perfectly competent and benevolent as we perhaps once supposed our actual father to be.

What attitude ought we to take up, in view of this situation?

It would be senseless to be rebellious, since there is no god to rebel against. It would be wrong to let disappointment or terror or apathy or folly overcome us. It would be wrong to be sad or sarcastic or cynical or indignant. . . .

No; in a dark and cloudy day a book of humour is better than **The Shropshire Lad;** and one of the important parts of 'training for ill' is to acquire cheerfulness.

Cheerfulness is part of courage, and courage is an essential part of the right attitude. Let us not tell ourselves a comforting tale of a father in heaven because we are afraid to be alone, but bravely and cheerfully face whatever appears to be the truth.

The theist sometimes rebukes the pleasure-seeker by saying: *We were not put here to enjoy ourselves; man has a sterner and nobler purpose than that.'* The atheist's conception of man is, however, still sterner and nobler than that of the theist. According to the theist we were put here by an all-powerful and all-benevolent god who will give us eternal victory and happiness if we only obey him. According to the atheist our situation is far sterner than that. There is no one to look after us but ourselves, and we shall certainly be defeated.

As our situation is far sterner than the theist dares to think, so our possible attitude towards it is far nobler than he conceives. When we contemplate the friendless position of man in the universe, as it is right sometimes to do, our attitude should be the tragic poet's affirmation of man's ideals of behaviour. Our dignity, and our finest occupation, is to assert and maintain our own self-chosen goods as long as we can, those great goods of beauty and truth and virtue. And among the virtues it is proper to mention in this connection above all the virtues of courage and love. There is no person in this universe to love us except ourselves; therefore let us love one another. The human race is alone; but individual men need not be alone, because we have each other. We are brothers without a father; let us all the more for that behave brotherly to each other. The finest achievement for humanity is to recognize our predicament, including our insecurity and our coming extinction, and to maintain our cheerfulness and love and decency in spite of it. We have good things to contemplate and high things to do. Let us do them.

We need to create and spread symbols and procedures that will confirm our intentions without involving us in intellectual dishonesty. This need is urgent today. For we have as yet no strong ceremonies to confirm our resolves except religious ceremonies, and most of us cannot join in religious ceremonies with a good conscience. When the *Titanic* went down, people sang 'nearer, my God, to thee'. When the Gloucesters were in prison in North Korea they strengthened themselves with religious ceremonies. At present we know no other way to strengthen ourselves in our most testing and tragic times. Yet this way has become dishonest. That is why it is urgent for us to create new ceremonies, through which to find strength without falsehood in these terrible situations. It is not enough to formulate honest and high ideals. We must also create the ceremonies and the atmosphere that will hold them before us at all times. I have no conception how to do this; but I believe it will be done if we try.

ATHEISTS LOVE MANKIND

An Atheist loves his fellow man instead of a god. An Atheist believes that heaven is something for which we should work now, here on earth, for all men together to enjoy. An Atheist believes that he can get no help through prayer, but that he must find in himself the inner conviction and strength to meet life, to grapple with it, to subdue it and enjoy it. An Atheist believes that only in a knowledge of himself and a knowledge of his fellow man can he find the understanding that will help to a life of fulfillment.

He seeks to know himself and his fellow man, then, rather than to know a god. An Atheist believes that a hospital should be built instead of a church. An Atheist believes that a deed should be done instead of a prayer said. An Atheist strives for involvement in life and not escape into death. He wants disease conquered, poverty banished, war eliminated. He wants man to understand and love man. He wants an ethical way of life. He believes that we cannot rely on a god or channel action into prayer, nor hope for an end of troubles in a hereafter. He believes that we are our brothers' keepers; *but more important,* we are the keepers of our own lives; that we are responsible persons and that the job is here and the time is now.

Murray v. Curlett, United States Supreme Court, 373 U.S. 179.

ALTERNATIVE **6**

THE PHILOSOPHY OF
TEILHARD DE CHARDIN

by John Kobler*

Mr. Kobler is a free lance writer who has contributed to **Life, New Yorker, Saturday Evening Post, Colliers** and other publications. He is the author of several books and has worked on the editorial staffs of **Life** and **Saturday Evening Post.**

The following questions should help you examine the reading:

1. In Teilhard's view, what major stages has evolution already gone through and what stage lies ahead?
2. Why could Teilhard's view of evolution be called an optimistic one?
3. What is Teilhard's "Law of Complexity-Consciousness"?

*John Kobler, *The Priest Who Haunts the Catholic World*, **Saturday Evening Post**, October 12, 1963, pp.44-46. Reprinted by permission of **The Saturday Evening Post**. © 1963, by the Curtis Publishing Company, and by permission of the author.

Pierre Teilhard de Chardin, who died in New York in 1955, was born in Auvergne, France in 1881. His major contribution has been his theory that brings together the fields of science and religion. He was a Jesuit priest whose writings were suppressed by the Roman Catholic Church  because they were considered contradictory to its official doctrines. He was also a noted geologist and theologian and one of the foremost palentologists of the twentieth century. Among other accomplishments, he was the co-discoverer of Peking Man, one of the earliest known hominids or manlike creatures.

In his major work, **The Phenomenon of Man**, Teilhard

> depicts evolution as the progress of the universe — a progress divinely conceived and therefore irresistible — from elemental matter through the advent of life, animal consciousness and human thought toward God. "Man did not descend from an ape," he was fond of saying. "He ascended."*

In addition to **The Phenomenon of Man**, Teilhard has written many other books which have been published around the world since his death. Some of these are **The Divine Milieu, Vision of the Past, Man's Place in Nature, Hymn of the Universe** and **The Future of Man**.

*IBID., p. 44.

Catholic dogma does not require believers to accept Genesis literally. It permits a variety of theories, including evolution, providing they recognize Scripture as divine revelation. Fifteen centuries ago Saint Augustine advised Christians not to consider the Bible a scientific text, and his own commentary on Genesis is often cited to show that evolution can be compatible with orthodoxy. Nevertheless, in practice evolution has long been a risky area for Catholics, because its early proponents were predominantly materialists who dismissed God from the universe. In fact, not until Pope Pius XII's encyclical letter of 1950, *Humani Generis,* did the church explicitly authorize Catholic scholars to explore evolution, and then only as an unproven hypothesis.

In Teilhard's system, however, evolution is no hypothesis. It is the key to the whole meaning of existence. It operates not through blind chance as the scientific materialists argued, but purposefully, an irreversible process planned by God. A twofold principle underlies this process: Nothing can appear that has not been prepared from all eternity, and the universe is always at work perfecting itself.

Every process of material growth in the Universe is ultimately directed towards spirit, and every process of spiritual growth is ultimately directed towards Christ.

Pierre Teilhard de Chardin in **Science and Christ**.

The starting point of evolution from primordial matter Teilhard called Alpha, and the Goal, the Omega Point. Omega is, in effect, God, but Alpha also contains God. Thus, the universe began in God and will return to Him. *"Man,"* Teilhard wrote, *"is not a static center of the world, as he long assumed, but the axis and arrow of evolution, which is something finer."* So far the march of evolution has advanced through three major stages — pre-life, life and thought. Hyper-life, for which Teilhard believed man to be now ripe, lies ahead. *". . . humanity has just entered what is probably the greatest transformation it has ever known. . . . Something is happening in the structure of human consciousness. It is another species of life that is just beginning."*

TEILHARD'S VIEW OF EVOLUTION

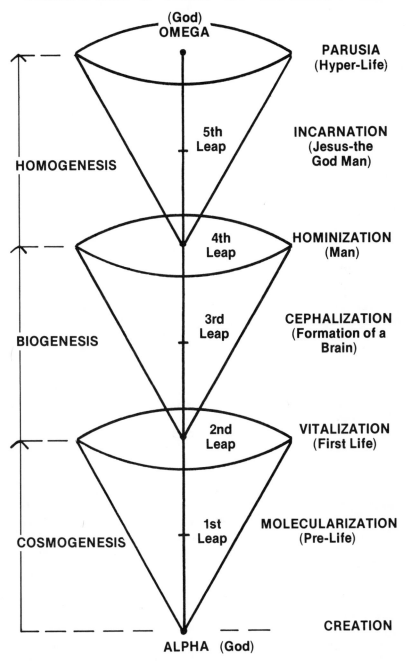

(God)
OMEGA

PARUSIA
(Hyper-Life)

5th
Leap

INCARNATION
(Jesus-the
God Man)

HOMOGENESIS

4th
Leap

HOMINIZATION
(Man)

3rd
Leap

CEPHALIZATION
(Formation of a
Brain)

BIOGENESIS

2nd
Leap

VITALIZATION
(First Life)

1st
Leap

MOLECULARIZATION
(Pre-Life)

COSMOGENESIS

CREATION

ALPHA (God)

Diagram by editor.

55

From hyper-life, Teilhard prophesied, with the boundless optimism that colored his vision, humanity individually and collectively will eventually enter into ultimate, perfect union with God at the Omega Point, and so will conclude the epic drama of evolution. Nothing, he felt, could prevent that final consummation.

As the main forces of evolution, Teilhard posited two kinds of energy. The first kind, "tangential" energy, acts upon what he termed the *"Outside of Things."* Scientists see the growth of the universe as a sequence of combinations: atoms forming molecules, molecules forming cells, cells forming plants and animals.

But the physical and chemical forces that bring about these changes manufacture no new energy. According to the laws of thermodynamics, the new organism expends its energy in heat and eventually disintegrates. Physicists reckon that the sun, for example, will consume all its available hydrogen atoms in about 15 billion years, then cool off and die. *"A rocket rising in the wake of time's arrow that bursts only to be extinguished,"* Teilhard reflected poetically, *"an eddy rushing on the bosom of a descending current — such then must be our picture of the descending current — such then must be our picture of the world. So says science, and I believe in science, but up to now has science ever troubled to look at the world except from without?"*

Teilhard rejected the prospect of the universe thus reduced to a cold, black void, of evolution vanquished. God, he believed, could not have intended such an end of his creation. There must exist some other kind of energy capable of producing higher forms ad infinitum and thereby preventing universal decay. Teilhard looked for such an energy on the *"Inside of Things,"* by which he meant consciousness to even the lowest forms of inorganic matter. Operating on the Inside, on consciousness, he concluded, was a *"radial"* or spiritual energy, separate from but related to tangential energy. Reversing the laws of thermodynamics, he formulated the *"Law of Complexity-Consciousness."*

According to this law, complexity increases on the Outside until stopped by the loss of tangential energy. But on the Inside, radial energy, which is inexhaustible, drives the organism toward higher levels of both complexity and consciousness. In the evolution of animals, complexity-consciousness reached the level of instinct and awareness, in man, the level of thought, moral judgment, freedom of choice, spiritually. *"Animals merely know,"* said Teilhard, *"but man knows he knows."* Since radial energy is a tremendous reservoir, it will go on producing more and more complex forms and so outdistance the rate of atomic disintegration.

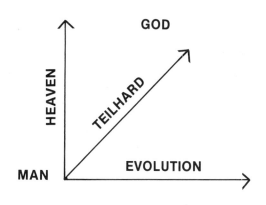

IMPROVING MAN'S CONDITION

HEAVEN — Most religions promise a reward after death for a life well spent.

EVOLUTION — Some scientists, skeptical of a divine presence in history, claim that man's hope for the future lies in improving his surroundings, and more importantly, himself.

TEILHARD — There is a source of energy in man, divinely implanted, that propels man forward and upward, physically, mentally and spiritually.

Diagram by editor. For Teilhard's version see page 269 of **Future of Man**, Harper and Row edition, 1964.

Through this interplay of the Outside and the Inside, Teilhard reinterpreted evolution, the universe and God. Geologists describing the successive layers of the earth speak of the barysphere, composed of metals; the lithosphere, of rocks; the hydrosphere, of water. Teilhard invented a new layer, the noosphere (from the Greek *noos:* mind). Thought, he explained, generated the noosphere. *"The idea is that of the earth not only becoming covered by myriads of grains of thought but becoming enclosed in a single thinking envelope so as to form, functionally, no more than a single vast grain of thought. . . ."*

But the noosphere is not the apex of evolution. Beyond it, Teilhard believed, beckons a further series of syntheses converging toward the Omega Point. The prerequisite to this final ascent is man's social consciousness. Just as aggregates of cells form an individual, so the aggregate of individuals will form a super-organism, a collective, combining the sum total of human consciousness. But how can personality and collectivity combine without damage to either? Teilhard finds the answer in a special property of radial energy — love. And the power that moves the universe through love toward the zenith is Christianity. In the culminating synthesis of evolution a universal consciousness, forever freed from material shackles, will fuse with Omega. . . .

DISTINGUISHING BETWEEN STATEMENTS THAT ARE PROVABLE AND THOSE THAT ARE NOT

From various sources of information we are constantly confronted with statements and generalizations about social and moral problems. In order to think clearly about these problems, it is useful if one can make a basic distinction between statements for which evidence can be found, and other statements which cannot be verified because evidence is not available, or the issue is so controversial that it cannot be definitely proved. Students should constantly be aware that social studies texts and other information often contain statements of a controversial nature. The following exercise is designed to allow you to experiment with statements that are provable and those that are not.

In each of the following statements indicate whether you believe it is provable (P), too controversial to be proved to everyone's satisfaction (C), or unprovable because of the lack of evidence (U). Compare and discuss your results with your classmates.

P = Provable
C = Too Controversial
U = Unprovable

____ 1. Organized religion, institutional churches, have been responsible for many of the positive developments of human culture.

____ 2. Organized religion, institutional churches, have hindered the development of mankind.

____ 3. Abortion is simply a case of murder.

____ 4. Abortions must be legalized if we are to combat overpopulation and survive on this planet.

____ 5. Habitual criminals lack a proper value structure.

____ 6. Everyone should attend a church of his choice frequently.

____ 7. America's churches should play a leading part in solving its racial problems.

____ 8. It is unconstitutional for public schools to schedule religion classes.

THE PHILOSOPHY
OF THE DOLLAR

by Robert L. Heilbroner*

Robert L. Heilbroner has approached the history of money and men's hunger for it through careful and scholarly analysis of what the great economists have written about business and society. His **The Worldly Philosophers** summed up fifteen years of economic study began at Harvard University. After taking his degree summa cum laude with a Phi Beta Kappa key, he combined practical work in both government and private business with further study at the New School for Social Research.

Use the following questions to assist you in your reading:

1. What does the author mean when he speaks of our society as an *"acquisitive society"*?
2. In the author's opinion, how does money stabilize our society?
3. What does the author mean when he says *"the values of an acquisitive society have a metallic sound"*? Do you agree?

---

*Robert L. Heilbroner, **The Quest for Wealth** (New York: Simon and Schuster, 1956), pp. 3-26. Reprinted by permission of Simon and Schuster, Inc.

As far back as there is history, men have dreamed of wealth: to what heights have they not reached — and to what depths have they not sunk — in quest of those golden dreams! High treason and low trickery, great affairs of state and petty squabbles over an inheritance, marriage and murder: what aspect of the tragicomedy of man has not been touched by the love of gain? Truly the drive for riches must be adjudged as powerful and protean a stimulus as any to which the human mechanism responds. . . .

There is a psychological trait of *possessiveness* or *projection*, which seems to be a universal human characteristic (except in severely disturbed personalities which have little or no relation to the world whatsoever). It is, if we wish to call it so, an *"instinct,"* although *"capacity"* would seem to be a more descriptive word. Possessiveness, however, is not "acquisitiveness"; the former consists only in imbuing the surrounding world with a living reflection of the self — with making that world, in some intensely real if unrealistic fashion, part of one's self. In order for the acquisitive impulse to manifest itself, one more step must be taken. The individual must act "acquisitively" — collectingly, if you will — toward that animated outer world. He must use the endowment of his projective personality in an acquisitive fashion for the satisfaction of his needful ego. . . .

Let us begin with a look at an acquisitive society — our own. What does it mean that we live in an acquisitive world? The words would seem to imply that we are all strivers after grandiose riches, or that we are all — however politely concealed — tinged with avarice and greed. And yet we are obviously not; indeed, if we are to trust the current sociologists it is not riches we seek but security, not problematical luxury but assured comfort, not self-aggrandizement but self-effacement in conformtiy. Everyone still claims he would like to have *"a million dollars,"* but one suspects that not a few would actually be happier with an inconspicuous income of ten thousand.

> **The values of an acquisitive society have a metallic flavor. Money is sought not only for the needs of life but as an end, good in itself.**

But there is a difference between acquisitiveness in the sense of a personal consuming desire for wealth and the generalized acquisitiveness of a society such as our own. An acquisitive person is one whose psyche is gratified by the accumulation of wealth; an acquisitive society is one whose continuity is assured by the use of wealth as an incentive. Reduced to its essentials, it is a society oriented around money.

What does such an orientation mean? To begin with it implies a technical fact: that society attends to its daily provisioning by a system of money rewards and money penalties. It is a society in which all are bound together in an omnipresent web of money, buying and selling not only the goods on a marketplace but the services and labor which must produce those goods in the first place. A money-run society dispenses with authoritarian commands and tradition both; it sows its seed, mines its ore and performs the thousand and one interlocking tasks of survival through

a dependence of the efficacy of monetary stimuli. In a money-run society we must make money to live, and although the amount we make may be very small we are nonetheless necessitously engaged in its pursuit.

Furthermore, we are engaged in its pursuit for more than the actual necessaries of life. The clerk in the grocery store and the worker on the assembly line might protest that they are not questing for wealth but for a livelihood — as indeed they are. Yet even at this lowest echelon, something of the unsatisfied drive for wealth has trickled down. For the *values* of an acquisitive society have a metallic flavor. Money is sought not only for the needs of life but as an end, good in itself.

Thus, how does the clerk or the man on the assembly line commonly judge which of two jobs — perhaps jobs far above his head — is the "better"? Not so much by comparing their respective tasks as by asking which one pays the more. How does he judge which of two men is the more "successful"? Rarely by inquiring into their private lives, but by inquiring into their incomes. Or how does he distinguish a "good" business from a "poor" one? Not by evaluating technological achievements or community relations or social importance, but by noting their respective profit statements. . . .

Thus the hallmark of an acquisitive society is that a society not only contains acquisitive personalities (as perhaps do all societies) but that it harnesses the acquisitive propensity to a social end. On the purely practical side it controls the flow of goods from hand to hand and the flow of people from job to job by monetary stimuli — if not in each instance, at least in the large. On the cultural side it sets up and encourages a standard of values in which money is the meaningful measure of much of life. An acquisitive society is not one which is necessarily dominated by avarice and greed — it may indeed be shot through, as is ours, with strong reservations about the morality of certain aspects of wealth. Nonetheless it is a society actuated by money, a society in which the quest for wealth, diffused throughout all its members, provides not only the main incentive to work but is regarded as the ordinary and proper measure of the value of almost all things. . . .

ALTERNATIVE **8**

COMMUNAL LIFE

by Michael Bennett*

This reading is the result of a visit by Michael Bennett, a reporter, to a commune in New York City called The Loft, to view its life style and interview its members.

Bring the following questions to your reading:

1. What is the purpose of The Loft and other communes?
2. What goals does The Loft intend for its members that cannot be as easily realized in conventional society?
3. One of the commune's members speaks of The Loft as an example of *"the compassionate revolution."* What does he mean?
4. What problems would you anticipate living at The Loft? What rewards?

*Michael Bennett, *The Alternative*, **The Mother Earth News**, September, 1970, pp. 32-34. Reprinted with permission from **Zygote** magazine in which this reading originally appeared.

"The Loft," as it is called by its denizens, is one of the rapidly growing number of city communes that have sprung up in New York and other urban conglomerates in recent years. As with most new endeavors, all the commune members are intent upon making it a success — a place where they will be free to express themselves and pursue their chosen interests, a central unit where they live and work together toward creating an alternative life-style.

I was very interested in understanding the workings of a city commune, realizing that if such a thing caught on in the huge metropolises of Amerika, that the whole idea and function of the city would change from a place which departmentalizes people to a place which brings people together harmoniously to work toward their common and individual goals.

The commune is a base from which to operate . . . There's no attempt to make everyone think, behave, act or get involved in the same type of things; this would be contrary to the nature of what we're trying to do . . . The commune itself is an experiment in life-style.

The Loft, according to Finley, an articulate and together member, *"is a widely diverse group of people in a highly pressurized urban situation . . . a kind of situation where everybody can get his own head together, his own talent together, his own interest together . . . really make them work the way he wants them to, and yet let the total thing flow as a very real organic community."* The word 'organic' means that the community will evolve in its own particular way, the variables being the people who live together. Laws in themselves will not be imposed, but will be organically developed to suit the needs of each person as well as the commune as a whole. . . .

I was first taken on a tour of the commune to get a sense of the physical layout, its possibilities and its limitations. The commune itself occupies two loft-sized floors in an old building on lower 2nd Avenue, Manhattan. The main floor contains a huge kitchen-dining area, with a table big enough to seat all 27 communards and various friends during meals. (There were also 6 cats and a rabbit.)

Richard Fairfield in **Communes USA: A Personal Tour.** *

Next to the kitchen is a living room area which has a few chairs, some floor cushions and sound equipment for entertainment. In another room is the office of the Earth People's Park organization, whose purpose is to get land for the people (all people). Just off that is the office of Negative Entropy, an organization begun by Paul, a biologist, Harry, an engineer, and Bruce, who are trying to get a government grant for their project of freezing foods without chemicals. Another project is concerned with cryogenics, or the freezing of bodies for life extension. This floor also has a huge general meeting room about the size of a large dance floor. There are four bathrooms, and the day we were there, a six-headed shower had just been installed.

Upstairs are the sleeping quarters; a communal room where several members of the commune sleep on floor mattresses; another large room is being partitioned off for private sleeping quarters. Dick, one of the communards, is a writer and described the situation this way:

***Communes USA: A Personal Tour**, Penguin Books, 1972, is a frank appraisal of many different kinds of communes across the country, including their goals and accomplishments. It has helpful bibliographies and appendices.

"Basically, when we started the commune, we tried to set up a private area and a communal area, a concept that hasn't worked out, to the best of my knowledge, in any other commune. Most communes are immediately walls down, and many people are put into a situation that they can't cope with . . . We went through this at many meetings . . . what it boiled down to is this — if people need private space, these people will be taken care of as well as those who need communal space."

The operation of a city commune is especially interesting to me because until recently, I had always identified communal living with being in the wood, getting back to nature.

"The commune is a base from which to operate . . . There's no attempt to make everyone think, behave, act or get involved in the same type of things; this would be contrary to the nature of what we're trying to do . . . The commune itself is an experiment in life-style."

Many communards foresee that the communizing now taking place will eventually result in a nationwide network of communes in both the cities and the country. The people at The Loft are currently involved in the Alternate U's group on communes, where knowledge and resources of all communes can be pooled to make the communal operations of each flow more smoothly. They are hoping to get together several city communes and approach farmers and offer them complete purchase of their crops if they grow only organic foods.

If this is successful, such an arrangement could be expanded to a national scale; sympathetic farmers who don't want to screw up their soil with chemicals, as well as people living and working on country communes, could grow exclusively organic crops in order to supply the city communes and themselves. In this way, the communes could establish themselves as a self-sufficient society, at least as far as the basics are concerned. The success of this large-scale project would be enormously valuable as a living, working illustration that people only have to work to live and to help others live.

This could also lead to exchange programs between city and country communes. Members of a city commune go to a country commune and vice-versa for periods of time to help run the respective communes that they are visiting. People in the city would then be educated in the fundamentals of farming and country life, and the country people could come to the city to get themselves together in ways which require the resources the city has to offer.

The educational value of a commune setup is also enormous. For children, there will be no repression of their ideas and instincts. Tools will be available as the new life-style creates a new technology aimed towards self-fulfillment rather than production.

Before starting the commune, the founders met several times with the Hog Farmers to discuss the problems that would arise in the formative stages. They told me that in spite of the rapping, they still went through pretty much the same changes that the Hog Farm had gone through in getting itself together. Finley said:

"I don't think you can learn anything except from gut-level experience . . . so we always repeat the same mistakes. Things get together for a couple of days and then start to come apart . . . people realize the crisis and get it together again . . . But each time we go through a crisis we come together a little more . . . we begin to think of some free, but viable, orderly way to make our existence work . . . Anybody who doesn't want to do something . . . that should be OK . . . If they don't want to come to meetings, they can work in the kitchen . . . the totality will flow together . . ." The general feeling was . . . *"when you see something has to be done, you do it."*

Larry Speed Freak, who greeted us at the door with a torrent of words which were mostly un-understandable, described the reason for the commune: *"The purpose of people getting together like this is so each person can do his own thing and teach his thing to other people . . . Like, you can learn more in a place like this than in any other place in the world, because you have somebody here who knows how to do something else . . . I'm a photographer. Pedro puts up bubbles. He helped construct the one at Union Square on Earth Day, and is currently involved in the design and construction of inflatables. . . .*

More generally, the purpose of the commune and of communes is to create an alternative society. In this sense, communes are to some degree political. Because the purpose of the commune is to eliminate the formal structures that keep us compartmentalized, these politics are of a different ilk than the politics we are so used to.

". . . We are opposed, in principle, to ideologics. We want good relationships with any group that is in any way

making a contribution towards constructive changes in society . . . We're primarily concerned with finding creative ways and effective means, which is where both the arts and sciences come into our trip. For us, it is essentially a creative revolution; with the creative imagination you can solve every problem that arises, and you can alter your course of action any time you encounter resistance to it. The imagination can think up one or a number of alternatives so you can always keep moving . . . If you have one ideology and a plan of action and one of those are blocked, then the movement is stopped . . . So creativity is not only a means for the Revolution, it is the ultimate style of life for us, too . . . which is why we're interested in artists and technolo-

71

gists being able to do their thing here. The one thing that everybody has in common, whether they're artists or scientists, is that they're looking for an alternative life that is more creative, more together, more fully human . . . more real."

It was stressed that this 'alternative' had to be open to everyone, from acid freaks to corporation executives. Everyone should be able to see that there is a better way to live than the way they are living now. The commune will be the place where art and technology complement one another; artist, writer, biologist, typist et al. will unite in common human endeavors, learning from each other, rather than boxed into isolated specialties. . . .

On a personal, as well as a communal level, there are several problems which are implicit in so many people living together. One of the most obvious is the problem of privacy. As one of the communards already mentioned, The Loft is set up for private quarters as well as communal quarters, depending on each person's needs. *"When I feel that I want to be alone, it just happens, you know, people are really sensitive to me, and I'm sensitive to them."* As it turns out, most of the communards find that if they need to be alone there is usually someplace they can go, and if things are really too hectic, they leave the commune for a while.

They don't see the need for privacy impinging on them; it doesn't happen often, and more important, no one really gets uptight when it does happen.

Another problem is finances. Right now, because the building is in shoddy condition, there is not any rent to be paid. Some of the members have jobs on the outside; some are artists and writers and they make bread that way when they need it. Everyone, however, spends a good deal of time working on the commune, preparing the private living quarters, building things. Another room, off the living quarters, is in a state of total disarray; eventually, they plan to rebuild it as a biology laboratory and a darkroom. This takes bread and everyone contributes what they can. Surprisingly, there is enough money now to do what must be done, and the rule that each person has to contribute $50 a month has not had to be enforced. Some people have put in a lot more, some a lot less. If money does become a problem, they'll cope when the time comes.

Many communes have been troubled by crashers who are not a part of the commune. Ideally, there would be accommodations for visitors, but due to the lack of space, some restrictions may be necessary. Pedro said *"It depends on your mood — sometimes you get mad at everybody and throw everybody out . . . sometimes it's OK."* Sara: *"Somebody who isn't welcome here wouldn't want to stay"*; Finley: *"Opinions vary from people who feel that all doors should be open all the time to those who feel all doors should be closed as far as private living space is concerned. Friends are helpful once we can get ourselves together . . . When we're not together, the ideas of other people only make confusion. Problems are worked out by virtue of living together and the process of caring for each other. This is the compassionate revolution."* . . .

PREDICTING AND
EVALUATING RESPONSES

Much is made of the generation gap, one cause of which is the tendency of young and old to value actions and goals differently. This exercise provides the opportunity to discuss, analyze, and predict how the generations (let us cite two for the purpose of discussion, those over thirty, and those under thirty) would construct different value scales from the same set of choices.

From the following list of choices, list the five you believe the younger generation values most, assigning the number (1) to the value you believe it would consider most important, the number (2) to the second most important, and so on, until you have completed five choices. Rank five choices for the older generation also. Discuss your rankings with the class. Give your reasoning for the choices you have made and listen to the reasons your classmates present for the choices they have made.

Choices

(A) Respect for elders and those in authority
(B) Proper dress, manners and deportment
(C) Personal freedom
(D) Economic independence
(E) Love as the motive for actions
(F) Fulfillment of commitments and responsibilities
(G) Complete openness and acceptance of others
(H) Work that is productive
(I) Work that is self-fulfilling
(J) Loyalty to country

Younger Generation

1st Choice _____ why?

2nd Choice _____ why?

3rd Choice _____ why?

4th Choice _____ why?

5th Choice _____ why?

Older Generation

1st Choice _____ why?

2nd Choice _____ why?

3rd Choice _____ why?

4th Choice _____ why?

5th Choice _____ why?

74

ALTERNATIVE 9

THE HINDU VIEW OF LIFE

by Sir Sarvepalli Radhakrishnan*

Sir Sarvepalli Radhakrishnan, an Indian born in 1888, has had a long and amazingly productive career. In addition to being a philosopher and the author of numerous books, many dealing with religion, he has taught religion and ethics at Oxford, represented India as its ambassador to the U.S.S.R., been Chancellor of Delhi University, and served as Vice-President of his country.

Consider the following questions while reading:

1. How does Hinduism differ from Western religions?
2. How does Hinduism attempt to define God?
3. Some claim, that more than most religions, Hinduism exemplifies the virtue of an open mind. How does this reading seem to help justify this observation?

*Sir Sarvepalli Radhakrishnan, **The Hindu View of Life** (New York: The Macmillan Company, 1926), pp. 15-52. Reprinted with permission from The Macmillan Company.

The Hindu attitude to religion is interesting. While fixed intellectual beliefs mark off one religion from another, Hinduism sets itself no such limits. Intellect is subordinated to intuition, dogma to experience, outer expression to inward realization. Religion is not the acceptance of academic abstractions or the celebration of ceremonies, but a kind of life or experience. It is insight into the nature of reality (darsana), or experience of reality (anubhava). This experience is not an emotional thrill, or a subjective fancy, but is the response of the whole personality, the integrated self to the central reality. Religion is a specific attitude of the self, itself and no other, though it is mixed up generally with intellectual views, aesthetic forms, and moral valuations. . . .

The Hindu thinker readily admits other points of view than his own and considers them to be just as worthy of attention. If the whole race of man, in every land, of every colour, and every stage of culture is the offspring of God, then we must admit that, in the vast compass of his providence, all are being trained by his wisdom and supported by his love to reach within the limits of their powers a knowledge of the Supreme.

The chief sacred scriptures of the Hindus, the Vedas, register the intuitions of the perfected souls.[1] They are not so much dogmatic dicta as transcripts from life. They record the spiritual experiences of souls strongly endowed with the sense for reality. They are held to be authoritative on the ground that they express the experiences of the experts in the field of religion. If the utterances of the Vedas were uninformed by spiritual insight, they would have no claim to our belief. The truths revealed in the Vedas are capable of being re-experienced on compliance with ascertained conditions. . . .

The Hindu philosophy of religion starts from and returns to an experimental basis. Only this basis is as wide as human nature itself. Other religious systems start with this or that particular experimental datum. Christian theology, for example, takes its stand on the immediate certitude of Jesus as one whose absolute authority over conscience is self-certifying and whose ability and willingness to save the soul it is impossible not to trust. Christian

[1] Taittiriya Aranyaka, i. 2.

theology becomes relevant only for those who share or accept a particular kind of spiritual experience, and these are tempted to dismiss other experiences as illusory and other scriptures as imperfect. Hinduism was not betrayed into this situation on account of its adherence to fact. The Hindu thinker readily admits other points of view than his own and considers them to be just as worthy of attention. If the whole race of man, in every land, of every colour, and every stage of culture is the offspring of God, then we must admit that, in the vast compass of his providence, all are being trained by his wisdom and supported by his love to reach within the limits of their powers a knowledge of the Supreme. When the Hindu found that different people aimed at and achieved God-realization in different ways, he generously recognized them all and justified their place in the course of history. He used the distinctive scriptures of the different groups for their uplift since they remain the source, almost the only source, for the development of their tastes and talents for the enrichment of their thought and life, for the appeal to their emotions and the inspiration of their efforts. . . .

It is sometimes urged that the descriptions of God conflict with one another. It only shows that our notions are not true. To say that our ideas of God are not true is not to deny the reality of God to which our ideas refer. Refined definitions of God as moral personality, and holy love may contradict cruder ones which look upon Him as a primitive despot, a sort of sultan in the sky, but they all intend the same reality. . . .

When asked to define the nature of God, the seer of the Upanisad sat silent, and when pressed to answer exclaimed that the Absolute is silence. santa 'yam atma. The mystery of the divine reality eludes the machinery of speech and symbol. The *"Divine Darkness,"* *"That of which nothing can be said,"* and such other expressions are used by the devout when they attempt to describe their consciousness of direct communion with God.

The Hindu thinkers bring out the sense of the otherness of the divine by the use of negatives, *"There the eye goes not, speech goes not, nor mind, we know not, we understand not how one would teach it."*[2] . . .

---

[2] Kena Up., 3.

The unity of religions is to be found in that which is divine or universal in them and not in what is temporary and local. Where there is the spirit of truth there is unity. As in other matters, so in the sphere of religion there is room for diversity and no need for discord. To claim that any one religious tradition bears unique witness to the truth and reveals the presence of the true God is inconsistent with belief in a living God who has spoken to men "by diverse portions and in diverse manners."[20] God is essentially self-communicative[21] and is of ungrudging goodness, as Plato taught.[22] There is no such thing as a faith once for all delivered to the saints. Revelation is divine-human. As God does not reveal His Being to a stone or a tree, but only to men, His revelation is attuned to the state of the human mind. The Creative Spirit is ever ready to reveal Himself to the seeking soul provided the search is genuine and the effort intense. The authority for revelation is not an Infallible Book or an Infallible Church but the witness of the inner light. What is needed is not submission to an external authority but inward illumination which, of course, is tested by tradition and logic. If we reflect on the matter deeply we will perceive the unity of spiritual aspiration and endeavor underlying the varied upward paths indicated in the different world faiths. The diversity in the traditional formulations tends to diminish as we climb up the scale of spiritual perfection. All the paths of ascent lead to the mountaintop.

Sarvepalli Radhakrishnan in **This Is My Philosophy**, edited by Whit Burnett.

Hindu thought believes in the evolution of our knowledge of God. We have to vary continually our notions of God until we pass beyond all notions into the heart of the reality itself, which our ideas endeavour to report. Hinduism does

[20]Epistle to the Hebrews 1:1.

[21]**Bhagavadgita**, IV, 3.

[22]**Timaeus**, 29B.

not distinguish ideas of God as true and false, adopting one particular idea as the standard for the whole human race. It accepts the obvious fact that mankind seeks its goal of God at various levels and in various directions, and feels sympathy with every stage of the search. The same God expresses itself at one stage as power, at another as personality, at a third as all-comprehensive spirit, just as the same forces which put forth the green leaves also cause the crimson flowers to grow. We do not say that the crimson flowers are all the truth and the green leaves are all false. Hinduism accepts all religious notions as facts and arranges them in the order of their more or less intrinsic significance. The bewildering polytheism of the masses and the uncompromising monotheism of the classes are for the Hindu the expressions of one and the same force at different levels. Hinduism insists on our working steadily upwards and improving our knowledge of God. *"The worshippers of the Absolute are the highest in rank; second to them are the worshippers of the personal God; then come the worshippers of the incarnations like Rama, Krsna, Buddha; below them are those who worship ancestors, deities and sages, and lowest of all are the worshippers of the petty forces and spirits."*[3] Again, *"The deities of some men are in water* (i.e. bathing-places), *those of the more advanced are in the heavens, those of the children* (in religion) *are in images of wood and stone, but the sage finds his God in his deeper self."*[4] *"The man of action finds his God in fire, the man of feeling in the heart, and the feeble-minded in the idol, but the strong in spirit find God everywhere."*[5] *The seers see the Supreme in the self, and not in images. . . .*

Hinduism developed an attitude of comprehensive charity instead of a fanatic faith in an inflexible creed. It accepted the multiplicity of aboriginal gods and others which originated, most of them outside the Aryan tradition, and justified them all. It brought together into one whole all believers in God. Many sects professing many different beliefs live within the Hindu fold. Heresy-hunting, the favourite game of many religions, is singularly absent from Hinduism.

[3] upasana brahmanah prak, dvitiya sagunasya ca
  trtiya smaryate lilavigrahopasana budhaih
  upantya pitrdevarsigananam astyupasana
  antima ksudradevanam pretadinam vidhiyate.

[4] apsu deva manusyanam divi deva manisinam
  balanam kasthalosthesu buddhasy atmani devata.

[5] agnau kriyavato devo hrdi devo manisinam
  pratimasv alpabuddhinam jnaminam sarvatah sivah.

Hinduism is wholly free from the strange obsession of the Semitic faiths that the acceptance of a particular religious metaphysic is necessary for salvation, and nonacceptance thereof is a heinous sin meriting eternal punishment in hell. . . .

After all, what counts is not creed but conduct. By their fruits ye shall know them and not by their beliefs. Religion is not correct belief but righteous living.[6] The truly religious never worry about other people's beliefs. Look at the great sayng of Jesus: *"Other sheep I have which are not of this fold."* Jesus was born a Jew and died a Jew. He did not tell the Jewish people among whom he found himself, *"It is wicked to be Jews. Become Christians."* He did his best to rid the Jewish religion of its impurities. He would have done the same with Hinduism were he born a Hindu. The true reformer purifies and enlarges the heritage of mankind and does not belittle, still less deny it.

Those who love their sects more than truth end by loving themselves more than their sects. We start by claiming that Christianity is the only true religion and then affirm that Protestantism is the only true sect of Christianity, Episcopalianism the only true Protestantism, the High Church the only true Episcopal Protestant Christian religion, and our particular standpoint the only true representation of the High Church view.

The Hindu theory that every human being, every group and every nation has an individuality worthy of reverence is slowly gaining ground. Such a view requires that we should allow absolute freedom to every group to cultivate what is most distinctive and characteristic of it. All peculiarity is unique and incommunicable, and it will be to disregard the nature of reality to assume that what is useful to one will be useful to everyone else to the same extent. The world is wide enough to hold men whose natures are different. . . .

THE HINDU

EIGHT-SPOKED

WHEEL

[6]Cp. Spinoza: "Religion is universal to the human race; wherever justice and charity have the force of law and ordinance, there is God's kingdom."

ALTERNATIVE **10**

A SCIENTIST'S VIEW

by George Wald*

George Wald is a Harvard biology professor and Nobel Laureate in physiology medicine. He became nationally known following a talk he gave at Massachusetts Institute of Technology dealing with the influence of the military on American society. He is currently Higgins professor of biology.

Consider these questions before you approach the reading:

1. What does the author mean when he says he is a deeply religious person?
2. In the author's opinion, how did intelligent life originate on earth?
3. Why will we probably never make contact with other intelligent life in our galaxy and the universe?

*This reading is an edited version of a speech Mr. Wald delivered at the John XXIII Institute Conference on Theology and Ecology, St. Xavier College, Chicago, January 31, 1970. It is reprinted with the author's permission.

Man has been engaged, since we have known him, in an unending struggle to know: whence he comes, what kind of thing he is, and at least a hint of what may become of him.

I think that the struggle to know is epitomized in science. One could add a word and say an unending struggle to know God. I think the big question is, If one added that word, would one have changed the meaning of the sentence? For me, no.

I think of myself as a deeply religious person. But my religion is that of one scientist. It is wholly secular. It contains no supernatural elements. Nature is enough for me: enough of mystery, beauty, reality. I am getting along with nature. . . .

THE UNIVERSE AND MAN

We are not alone in this universe. We cannot be. I think we see now that if one begins a universe or any large part of it with just hydrogen, then in many places in it life will arise. Life arises in natural conditions by natural laws; and given enough time in any of those places, one will, I think, have achieved a thinking creature with a technology, like man — somewhat like man. . . .

As far as I can see, we are not by any means alone in this universe. It is a very big universe — so big that our own galaxy, the Milky Way, has the cozy feeling of being just our front yard. Yet that galaxy is almost unimaginably big. It takes light traveling at 186,000 miles a second over one hundred thousand years to cross the Milky Way. There are now about 3.5 billion people on this earth, and we are beginning to feel crowded; but there are one hundred billion stars like our sun in this galaxy, the Milky Way. A simple rule that is easy to remember in these matters of cosmology was stated by Eddington many years ago: 10^{11} stars make a galaxy (that is, one hundred billion; we are just a run-of-the-mill galaxy — they tend to be about that size); 10^{11} galaxies make a universe. The most conservative estimate I have seen of stars in the Milky Way with planets that might bear life is 1 percent. That makes one billion of them just in our own galaxy. They may not all have life, but given enough time they should. And of the one hundred billion galaxies that Eddington was talking about as making a universe, there are already roughly one billion within the range of our most powerful telescopes. One billion is 10^9. There are

SPONTANEOUS LIFE

Our planet is about 4.5 billion years old. About three billion years ago, life arose upon it. That was in the cards; it arose spontaneously. There was quite a controversy that disturbed scientists for a couple of centuries between the spontaneous and the supernatural creation of life. And there came a wonderful moment in this bitter controversy in which the champions on both sides were Catholic priests: an Italian priest, the Abbe Spallanzani, on the one side, insisting upon the impossibility of spontaneous generation, and, on the other side, as the great champion of spontaneous generation, John Turberville Needham, an English Jesuit, the founder and first president of the Belgian Royal Academy. I wondered how a priest could support the theory of spontaneous generation as opposed to its only conceivable alternative, supernatural creation. Needham tells us perfectly plainly that you have only to read the opening paragraphs of the Book of Genesis. The language used, at least in the first story of the creation, is not that God made the living creatures, but that he ordered the earth and waters to bring them forth. "Let the waters bring forth" those living things. "Let the earth bring forth" those living things. Needham's view was that, such orders having once been issued and never, as far as we know, rescinded, the earth and waters were forever free thereafter to bring forth life, which is exactly what we mean by spontaneous generation.

perhaps 10^9 planetary systems in our own galaxy capable of bearing life, many of which should have life; and there are 10^9 such galaxies already within range of observation; so it makes the fantastically large number of 10^{18} places in our already observed universe that are capable of bearing life.

It is almost unimaginable that in many of those places life must not have started long before it started here. How long before? You think of the pace that we have reached. What our world will be like if we can keep it going one hundred years from now almost transcends our capacities to imagine. But one hundred years is nothing. One thousand years is nothing. In geological time, one million years is just a day. There is no reason that we know of why, on planets elsewhere in our galaxy and in the universe, life should not have gotten going, and should not have gotten to that contemplative creature with a technology, very long before this — a million years, a hundred million years, perhaps even one billion years earlier.

These are hard thoughts. They make one ask the question, What then is our home in the universe? I think our home in the universe is the solar system — our corner of the universe. Let us talk about it a little. It is self-sufficient. Its source of energy is the sun. Relative to that, only negligible amounts of energy come in from the outside. I think the only life in the solar system is that on earth. Everything yet learned from the rockets, from space exploration, everything we have learned, is clinching that conviction: that the only life in the solar system is the life on earth. As for the position of man, I think that we are the only men in the universe. I have been talking about contemplative creatures who resemble man in their intellectual characteristics and in possessing a technology. But the chance that one of them is a man is negligible.

Man is the result of a long, long evolution, every step of which had a chance, a probability, of happening that way. Compound all those probabilities, and the chance of going through the operation just that way another time in another place is negligible. In fact, if you ask, Is there a chance that elsewhere in the universe there is a vertebrate — one of the great classes of vertebrates that include the fish, the amphibians, the reptiles, the birds, the mammals? I would say it is exceedingly unlikely, an almost negligible probability even for that.

So we have our own special individuality. That is true of the creatures here on this planet, including man, but also of the creatures in a reasonable well-inhabited galaxy and universe. And that, of course, raises a series of strange problems. One of them is, Are we ever going to come into contact — even into communication — with some advanced technological civilization in outer space? I myself think the chances are very small. For the distances are almost unimaginably great. If you ask the question, How far would you have to go to reach a sun — a star — that is of the right kind to have perhaps a planet that has a chance of containing life? I would tell you that the nearest one to my knowledge has the beautiful name of Epsilon Eridani — and it is 10.8 light years away. That is, it takes light traveling at 186,000 miles a second 10.8 years to get from us to Epsilon Eridani. That is how long it would take a radio message to travel that distance. And then, if there were someone on Epsilon Eridani to receive it, the probability of which is almost nil — we are asking not just for life, we are asking for someone who can receive radio messages — if there were such a creature, and if he realized that he were getting signals, and if he promptly responded, twenty-two years would have passed between our sending a signal and receiving a response — a long time. It would not make a lively conversation. That is the *nearest* possibility. The others are much farther out.

So are we likely to be visited? There has been all that talk that unidentified flying objects (UFOs) are perhaps visitors from outer space. There are two things against it. First of all, one would have to perform the trick of traveling close to the speed of light. It is hard to do that and not be light. And even that would make a very long journey. There is another matter that is a little amusng. There are one hundred billion solar systems just in our galaxy. If there even were creatures prepared to travel that way, why should they come here?

THE SCIENCE OF ASTROLOGY
WHY I BELIEVE IN ASTROLOGY

by Grant Lewi*

Mr. Lewi, who died in 1951, left the teaching of English at Dartmouth to study the science of astrology. He was at various times, the editor of **American Astrology** magazine, and the founder and editor of **The Astrologer**. The following reading is taken from his influential book **Astrology for the Millions**. He also wrote **Heaven Knows What**, a sequel to **Astrology for the Millions**, in 1935. Llewellyn Publications will publish an updated edition of **Heaven Knows What** in 1971.

The following questions should help your understanding of the reading:

1. How does Mr. Lewi react to the three chief reasons, that in his opinion, are generally advanced for not believing in astrology?
2. Why does he believe in astrology?

---

*Grant Lewi, **Astrology For The Millions** (St. Paul, Minn.: Llewellyn Publications, 1969), pp. 1-4. Reprinted with permission of Llewellyn Publications, P.O. Box 3383, St. Paul, Mn. 55101.

ASTROLOGY, bar sinister in the escutcheon of astronomy, maintains a unique and lonely position in human thought. It is "believed in" by a lot of people who know practically nothing about it; and it is "disbelieved in" by even more who know *absolutely* nothing about it.

Of no other art or science can this be said.

Astronomy, the haughty scientific offspring of astrology, has developed through the centuries into a science of celestial measurement. It has developed even further than the lay mind can comprehend, into a sort of metaphysics of time, space and motion which only initiates can talk about, let alone comprehend.

> **Mr. Halley: I don't believe in astrology!**
> **Sir Isaac Newton: Sir, I have studied the subject, you have not.**

Mathematics, intimately related to astronomy both through astrology and through the developments of centuries, has, like astronomy, grown with the ages into a part of the taken-for-granted language of our thinking.

Only the most stubborn and bigoted skeptic would think of standing up and saying, for example, that he *"did not believe in"* the Einstein theory, which is the most abstruse boundary to which astronomical and mathematical philosophy has reached. Such a skeptic would be promptly, and rightly, reprimanded by a more reasonable person, who would remind him that he was unequipped by information either to believe in, or disbelieve in, the Einstein theory.

Similarly, few will be found who have the temerity to "disbelieve" in the law of gravity, Avogadro's hypothesis, Newton's laws of motion, the multiplication table, the effect of sugar into the spinal column, Archimedes' principle, or the result of grafting sheep glands onto guinea pigs. These are not matters to "believe in" or "disbelieve in," but things to know about. Once you know, it is not necessary to believe; they are verifiable by experiment, and subject thereafter to the workings of law.

Astrology's position in human thought develops from the fact that it is frequently the subject of the most violent controversy, militantly carried on in the presence of practically no knowledge whatsoever.

Ask your doctor, for example, if he believes in astrology. Ten to one he will shake his head deprecatingly and say, *"Of course not!"*

If you ask him *"Why not?"* he will probably eye you suspiciously and reply something like, *"Don't tell me that an intelligent person like you believes in astrology!"*

At this point you must avow that you do not believe in astrology, you just were wondering about it. Thereupon, if he runs true to form, he will launch into a long discussion of why astrology must on the face of it be nonsense.

He will admit that, once upon a time, most of the world believed in astrology, but that was long ago, in the heyday of ignorance, before the dawn of science and the systematic search for truth. He will point out that astrology believes that the fate of men can be read in the stars; and he will go into a fine frenzy of righteous indignation that any modern could even consider such poppycock.

> **I have never heard of anyone who has investigated astrology and who has come away from his investigation dubbing it false. I should earnestly like to hear of such a person.**

Listen carefully to everything he says. See if you can detect one sound, scientific reason or proof that astrology is false. See if you can discover, among all the people you can find who *"don't believe in astrology,"* anyone who has a scientific or even a logical reason for not believing.

Three chief reasons are generally advanced for not believing in astrology: (1) It is superstition because it was believed in a superstitious age. This is not a superstitious age; therefore we should not believe in astrology. (2) It is perfectly ridiculous to believe that the planets can influence human beings. What! Those things millions of miles away?

88

Why it's absurd! (3) The Great Wizard Magipocus read my horoscope at a summer resort, and it was all wrong.

These are virtually all the arguments you will hear on the subject, so let's look at them carefully.

(1) It is superstition because it was believed in a superstitious age, etc. The great principles of mathematics and physics, none of them false, were laid down in the age of the world's youth and "superstition." Large portions of the *materia medica* were discovered by the ancients. The advanced astronomy of the Egyptians and Babylonians is well known; their calculations have been proved of phenomenal accuracy. These same intellectual and accurate ancients believed in astrology: surely this should be no part of the argument against it! The beliefs and findings of these same ancients which co-existed with their belief in astrology, and which have since been given the benefit of modern verification, have been proved amazingly true. It is plainly illogical to dub astrology *ipso facto* false because it was evolved by those same ancients who gave us the beginnings of astronomy, mathematics, physics, navigation, chemistry and medicine.

(2) It is perfectly ridiculous to believe that the planets could influence us! Now nothing, in itself, is "perfectly ridiculous to believe" — except something that goes against a known law of nature. In fact, all the laws we have of the solar system, with which astrology is concerned, tell us that it is quite logical to believe that every body of the solar system exerts a measurable, if small, influence on every other body. Thus it is not "perfectly ridiculous" at all to believe anything on faith alone; but it is equally ridiculous to disbelieve it on un-faith alone. Both faith and un-faith must bow before knowledge, of which, alas, woefully few people have any where astrology is concerned!

(3) Astrology must be false because so many astrologers are fakers. Well, if this were so, the law would be false because many lawyers are crooked; and medicine would be false because so many doctors are quacks and fee splitters. Architecture would be false because the Tower of Pisa leans; and art would be false because Diego Rivera painted Lenin instead of J.P. Morgan in Rockefeller Center.

There are many poor astrologers. There are many dishonest astrologers. There are many ignorant astrologers. There are many people reading and selling horoscopes who are not astrologers at all, but promoters, hack writers and petty racketeers.

A Llewellyn Publication

SIGNS	NAME	RULER	DETRIMENT	EXALTATION	FALL	GENDER	QUALITY	ATTRIBUTE	NATION	DIRECTION	ZONES
1 ARIES	RAM	♂ MARS	VENUS	SUN	SATURN	MASCULINE	BARREN	ARDOR	ENGLAND	MOVABLE	HEAD
2 TAURUS	BULL	♀ VENUS	MARS	MOON	URANUS	FEMININE	SEMI-FRUITFUL	STAMINA	PERSIA	FIXED	NECK
3 GEMINI	TWINS	☿ MERCURY	JUPITER	N.NODE	S.NODE	MASCULINE	BARREN	DIVERSITY	N.AMERICA	COMMON	ARMS
4 CANCER	CRAB	☽ MOON	SATURN	JUPITER	MARS	FEMININE	FRUITFUL	DEVOTION	HOLLAND	MOVABLE	BREAST
5 LEO	LION	☉ SUN	URANUS	NEPTUNE	URANUS	MASCULINE	BARREN	COURAGE	FRANCE	FIXED	HEART
6 VIRGO	VIRGIN	☿ MERCURY	NEPTUNE	MERCURY	VENUS	FEMININE	BARREN	PURITY	BRAZIL	COMMON	BOWELS
7 LIBRA	SCALES	♀ VENUS	MARS	SATURN	SUN	MASCULINE	SEMI-FRUITFUL	JUSTICE	JAPAN	MOVABLE	REINS
8 SCORPIO	SCORPION	♂ MARS	VENUS	URANUS	MOON	FEMININE	FRUITFUL	DESIRE	NORWAY	FIXED	SECRETS
9 SAGITTARIUS	ARCHER	♃ JUPITER	MERCURY	S.NODE	N.NODE	MASCULINE	SEMI-FRUITFUL	REASON	AUSTRALIA	COMMON	THIGHS
10 CAPRICORN	GOAT	♄ SATURN	MOON	MARS	JUPITER	FEMININE	SEMI-FRUITFUL	PRUDENCE	MEXICO	MOVABLE	KNEES
11 AQUARIUS	WATERMAN	♅ URANUS	SUN	URANUS	NEPTUNE	MASCULINE	BARREN	FELLOWSHIP	RUSSIA	FIXED	LEGS
12 PISCES	FISHES	♆ NEPTUNE	MERCURY	VENUS	MERCURY	FEMININE	FRUITFUL	SYMPATHY	PORTUGAL	COMMON	FEET

PLANETS	S	ORB	SIGNATURE AND NATURE OF THE PLANETS	DAY	TEMPERAMENT
1 SUN	☉	12°·17'	HOT DRY POWER HONOR FAME PRIDE INFLUENCE MASCULINE	SUNDAY	BENEFIC ●
2 MOON	☽	12°	COLD MOIST CHANGES PUBLIC AFFAIRS LIQUIDS BRAIN FEMININE	MONDAY	BENEFIC ●
3 MARS	♂	8°	HOT DRY DESIRE STRIFE FORCE ACTIVITY AMBITION PLUCK ARDENT	TUESDAY	MALEFIC ●
4 MERCURY	☿	8°	CONVERTABLE LITERATURE WRITINGS STUDY EXPRESSION MEMORY	WEDNESDAY	NEUTRAL ●
5 JUPITER	♃	10°	WARM MOIST JUDGEMENT PROFIT POWER GOOD FORTUNE HONESTY	THURSDAY	BENEFIC ●
6 VENUS	♀	8°	WARM PASSIVE PEACE JUSTICE ART GRACE FRUITFULLNESS MUSIC	FRIDAY	BENEFIC ●
7 SATURN	♄	8°	COLD HARD DRY CAUTION BINDING SORROW LOSS EFFORT SERIOUS	SATURDAY	MALEFIC ●
8 URANUS	♅	6°	COLD DRY AIRY OCCULT SCIENTIFIC ELECTRIC INVENTION AVIATION	WEDNESDAY	MALEFIC ●
9 NEPTUNE	♆	6°	NEUTRAL SPIRIT LIQUID CHEMICALS NARCOTICS SEANCES OIL GENIUS	FRIDAY	NEUTRAL ●

* Relative Terms only.

Yet this argument, like 1 and 2, is a phony, as any logical person can see.

Now in pointing out that these arguments — the clasics generally used against astrology — are not really arguments at all, I have not, of course, proved the truth of astrology. Far from it, I have merely tried to clear away the smoke of prejudice and confusion, in order that we may examine the subject on its own merits. It is the fashion today not to believe in astrology, just as long ago it was the fashion to believe in it.

Yet today, or yesterday, or tomorrow, intelligent people neither believe nor disbelieve something of which they are in total ignorance. When such a subject crosses their minds, they say, *"I don't know anything about it, and therefore can't have an opinion."* Then they are in a proper frame of mind to learn about it and thus acquire, not an opinion, not a belief, but a body of knowledge, from which the truth may appear.

Thus far, I have never heard of anyone who has investigated astrology and who has come away from his investigation dubbing it false. I should earnestly like to hear of such a person.

Richard Garnett, one-time curator of the British Museum, and a man of keen scientific bent, decided to study astrology to see what was in it. For his findings, I quote the 11th Edition Encyclopedia Britannica, Dr. Morris Jastrow's article on astrology:

> *Dr. Garnett insisted that it was a mistake to confuse astrology with fortune-telling, and maintained that it was a "physical science just as much as geology," depending like them on ascertained facts, and grossly misrepresented by being connected with magic.*

Isaac Newton, father of modern physics, reprimanded Mr. Halley who said to him, *"I don't believe in astrology"* with *"You have not studied the subject, sir; I have";* and Dr. Jastrow, concludes the Britannica article:

> *It is at least conceivable that some new synthesis might once more justify part, at all events, of ancient and medieval astrology.*

Men of good will, and of scientific bent, have thus far never been able to declare it false, have indeed seen in it the truth which eludes the mere skeptic whose knowledge of it is limited to a "belief".

My reasons for "believing in" astrology are extremely simple. I have studied it, I have put together known facts of people's lives with known planetary influences, and I have observed, in thousands of cases, correspondences which

91

BIOCOSMOLOGY OR COSMO-ECOLOGY*

In considering astrology, we may begin by recalling the origins of certain words. *Consider*, for example, is derived from the Latin *considerare*, "with the stars." A curiously parallel etymology is found in *desire*, originating the Latin *desiderare*, "from the stars." Thus, everyday language covertly contains the idea that the timing of our thoughts and our desires are somehow related to the stars. *Astronomy*, "the naming of stars," was originally a branch of *astrology*, the science of stars; until and including the times and teachings of Kepler and Newton, they were studied as one science. After the seventeenth century, that branch of the science which concerned itself with the study of the relationship of biological and psychological processes on earth with cosmic forces was driven underground and passed into the hands of unscientific fortune-tellers, whereas the increasingly precise quantitative measurement of planetary motion became separated from any concern with the effects of these motions on terrestrial life.

Two major areas of recent biological research are directly linked, however, with the forgotten science of astrology and promise to expand it in new and fruitful directions. First, ecology, the science of the inter-relations of life-forms and environments, when extended beyond the planet Earth, becomes the study of the reciprocally interacting solar and planetary field forces. It would be surprising indeed if there were no interaction effects in the system of sun and planets, balanced as exquisitely as the atomic system of nucleus and electrons. Secondly, the study of circadian rhythms in animals and man has gained increasing importance in the last decade and will undoubtedly expand to include the effects not only of the diurnal revolution of the Earth, but also of the orbits of sun, moon, and other planets. This new science will probably not be named *astrology*, since we are dealing primarily with the cycles of the planets, not the effects of stars in the modern sense, except for the sun. *Biocosmology* and *Cosmo-ecology* are among the terms which have been suggested.

*Footnight on following page.

are laws. I have watched these laws operate in the lives of individuals — of clients, of those close to me, of great men whose biographies are known or whose stories appear from day to day in the press of the contemporary world. I have watched Hitler and his chart, Roosevelt, Mussolini, Stalin; studied the careers and the charts of Napoleon, Bismarck, the old Kaiser, Lincoln, Washington, Wilson; as well as thousands of lesser individuals who, like yourself, respond to planetary action quite as much as do the great, the near-great, and the pseudo-great who for better and for worse make the headlines. The response of human beings to planetary stimuli is among the most amazing of all the natural phenomena capable of being observed.

I "believe in" astrology for the same reason that you "believe in" the multiplication table or the intoxicating effect of alcohol. It works!

*This is an excerpt from the article *Astrology: Potential Science & Intuitive Art*, by Ralph Metzner, which appeared in the August, 1970 issue of **Aquarian Agent**. Ralph Metzner is a psychologist whose main interests have been the exploration and mapping of consciousness. He has written **Maps of Consciousness** (Macmillan, 1971), which deals with astrology, the I Ching, the Tantras, the Tarot, alchemy and Agni Yoga (the Yoga of Fire). Reprinted with the author's permission.

FACT AND OPINION

This discussion exercise is designed to promote experimentation with one's ability to distinguish between fact and opinion. It is a fact, for example, that the United States was militarily involved in the Vietnam War. But to say this involvement served the interests of world peace is an opinion or conclusion. Future historians will agree that American soldiers fought in Vietnam, but their interpretations about the causes and consequences of the war will probably vary greatly.

Most of the following statements are taken from the readings in this book, some have other origins. Consider each statement carefully. Mark (O) for any statement you feel is an opinion or interpretation of the facts. Mark (F) for any statement you believe is a fact. Discuss and compare your judgments with those of other class members.

O = Opinion
F = Fact

( ) 1. The end always justifies the means.
( ) 2. The Bible contains the answers to many of man's problems.
( ) 3. God exists.
( ) 4. Sin is the cause of most of man's problems.
( ) 5. An absolute code of right and wrong exists, the difficulty is discovering it.
( ) 6. Catholicism has a legalistic moral code.
( ) 7. There is only one absolute moral law, to do the "loving thing" in every situation.
( ) 8. Atheism requires more courage than theism.*
( ) 9. Most value judgments in our society are made in terms of money.
( ) 10. A creative life is the ultimate style of living.
( ) 11. The Hindu concept of God is more correct than the Christian.
( ) 12. The Christian concept of God is more correct than the Hindu.
( ) 13. Astrology can indicate the pattern of the future.
( ) 14. Our solar system affects many functions of the human body.
( ) 15. Science has proved that traditional religions are ineffective and even harmful.

*Theism is the belief that there is a God.

A HUMANIST STATEMENT

by Corliss Lamont*

Corliss Lamont, a noted spokesman for humanism, received his Ph.D. in philosophy from Columbia in 1932. He is a member of Phi Beta Kappa and the American Humanist Association. He is also the author of several books, including **The Philosophy of Humanism, The Illusion of Immortality** and **The Independent Mind.**

Keep the following questions in mind as you read:

1. What is the position of humanism on the subject of God or the supernatural?
2. Why could humanists be called rationalists?
3. What is the author's position on ethics and sex?

*Corliss Lamont, *Naturalistic Humanism*, **The Humanist**, September-October, 1971, pp. 9-10. The original article has been slightly altered by the author for inclusion in this book. It is used with permission from **The Humanist** and the author.

Humanism is such a warm and attractive word that in the 20th century it has been adopted by various groups, often diametrically opposed in ideology, whose use of it is most questionable. Even the Catholics, who still adhere to every outworn myth of Christian supernaturalism, promote what they call *Catholic Humanism;* while the Marxists, who reject in practice political democracy and civil liberties, continually talk of *Socialist Humanism.*

But the Humanism that has become increasingly influential in this century, in English-speaking countries and throughout the non-Communist world, is *naturalistic Humanism.* This is the Humanism that I have supported through the written and spoken word for some 40 years.

To define naturalistic Humanism in a nutshell, it rejects all forms of supernaturalism, pantheism, and metaphysical idealism, and considers man's supreme ethical aim as working for the welfare of all humanity in this one and only life, using the methods of reason, science, and democracy for the solution of problems.

To become more specific, Humanism believes, **first**, that Nature or the universe makes up the totality of existence and is completely self-operating according to natural law, with no need for a God or gods to keep it functioning. This cosmos, unbounded in space and infinite in time, consists fundamentally of a constantly changing system of matter and energy, and is neutral in regard to man's well-being and values.

Second, Humanism holds that the race of man is the present culmination of a time-defying evolutionary process on this planet that has lasted billions of years; that man exists as an inseparable unity of mind and body, and that therefore after death there can be no personal immortality or survival of consciousness.

Third, in working out its basic views on man and the universe, Humanism relies on reason, and especially on the established facts, laws, and methods of modern experimental science. In general, men's best hope for solving their problems is through the use of intelligence and scientific method applied with vision and determination. Such qualities as courage, love, and perseverance provide emotional drive for successfully coping with difficulties, but it is reason that finds the actual solution.

Fourth, Humanism is opposed to all theories of universal determinism, fatalism, or predestination and believes

97

that human beings possess genuine freedom of choice (free will) in making decisions both important and unimportant. Free choice is conditioned by inheritance, education, the external environment (including economic conditions), and other factors. Nonetheless, it remains real and substantial. Humanism rejects both Marxist economic determinism and Christian theistic determinism.

Fifth, Humanism advocates an ethics or morality that grounds all human values in this-earthly experiences and relationships, and that views man as a functioning unity of physical, emotional, and intellectual faculties. The Humanist holds as his highest ethical goal the this-worldly happiness, freedom, and progress — economic, cultural, and material — of all mankind, irrespective of nation, race, religion, sex, or economic status. Reserving the word *love* for his family and friends, he has an attitude of *compassionate concern* toward his fellow men in general.

Sixth, in the controversial realm of sex relations, Humanism rejects entirely dualistic theories that separate soul from body and claim that the highest morality is to keep the soul pure and undefiled from physical pleasure and desire. The Humanist regards sexual emotions and their fulfillment as healthy, beautiful, and Nature's wonderful way of making possible the continued reproduction of the human race. While Humanism advocates high standards of conduct between the sexes, it rejects the puritanism of the past and looks upon sex love and sex pleasure as among the greatest of human experiences and values.

Seventh, Humanism believes that every individual must exercise a considerable amount of self-interest, if only to keep alive and healthy, but that altruistic endeavors on behalf of the community can be harmoniously combined with normal self-interest. Thus the good life is best attained by uniting the more personal satisfactions with important work and other activities that contribute to the welfare of one's city, nation, or other social unit. Significant work usually deepens a person's happiness.

Eighth, Humanism supports the widest possible development of the arts and the awareness of beauty, so that the aesthetic experience may become a pervasive reality in the life of men. The Humanist eschews the artifical distinction between the fine arts and the useful arts and asserts that the common objects of daily use should embody a fusion of utility and grace. The mass production of industrial goods by machinery need not necessarily de-

WHAT IS HUMANISM?

Humanism is the belief that man shapes his own destiny. It is a constructive philosophy, a non-theistic religion, a way of life.

Open-ended, without dogma, humanism is a world-view geared to our times. By focusing on the quality of each individual's life and stressing the need to work for social ideals, it fuses emotion and intellect.

Modern humanism has developed out of a growing respect for human dignity, for individual rights, and for the ideas of human equality, enthusiasm for life and for nature, recognition that ethical values grow out of experience, and feeling for humanity beyond one's national boundaries.

There are special challenges for the humanistic approach as we begin the 1970's. We must try to lessen the widening gap between technology and everyday experience, between current emphasis on living in the present and the need for foresight and planning. We must help each other recognize how everything has become interconnected. Ecological problems have become value problems. Regional problems are now world problems.

The Humanist relies upon himself and his fellow man rather than upon any supernatural power. He believes he can make headway in meeting difficulties by using intelligence and good will. He endeavors to become more tolerant and compassionate.

"I use the word 'Humanist' to mean someone who believes that man is just as much a natural phenomenon as an animal or plant; that his body, mind and soul were not supernaturally created but are products of evolution, and that he is not under the control or guidance of any supernatural being or beings, but has to rely on himself and his own powers." — **Julian Huxley**

American Humanist Association

feat this aim. Among other things, Humanism calls for the planned architectural reconstruction of towns and cities throughout America, so that beauty may prevail in our urban life.

Ninth, Humanism gives special emphasis to man's appreciation of the beauty and splendor of Nature. There is no heavenly Father in or behind Nature, but Nature is truly our fatherland. The Humanist energetically backs the widespread efforts for conservation, the protection of wild life, and the campaigns to maintain and extend ecological values. His keen responsiveness to every sort of natural beauty evokes in him a feeling of profound kinship with Nature and its myriad forms of life.

Tenth, for the actualization of human happiness and freedom everywhere on earth, Humanism advocates the establishment of international peace, democracy, and a high standard of living throughout the world. Humanists, in their concern for the welfare of all nations, peoples, and races, adopt William Lloyd Garrison's aphorism, "Our country is the world; our countrymen are all mankind." It follows that Humanists are strongly opposed to all forms of nationalist and racial prejudice.

Eleventh, Humanism believes that the best type of government is some form of political democracy, including civil liberties and full freedom of expression throughout all areas of economic, political, and cultural life. Reason and science are crippled unless they remain unfettered in the pursuit of truth. In the United States, the Humanist militantly supports the fundamental guarantees in the Bill of Rights.

Twelfth, Humanism, in accordance with scientific method, encourages the unending questioning of basic assumptions and convictions in every field of thought. This includes, of course, philosophy, naturalistic Humanism, and the 12 points I have outlined in this attempt at definition. Humanism is not a new dogma, but is a developing philosophy ever open to experimental testing, newly discovered facts, and more rigorous reasoning.

I do not claim that every Humanist will accept all of the 12 points I have suggested. There will be particular disagreement, I imagine, on the fourth point; that is, the one concerning free choice.

Not every Humanist wants to use the phrase *naturalistic* Humanism. Some prefer the term *scientific*

Humanism, *secular* Humanism, or *democratic* Humanism. There is also a large group who consider Humanism a *religion* and who find an institutional home in the Fellowship of Religious Humanists, with its quarterly journal, **Religious Humanism**. For my own part, I prefer to call naturalistic Humanism a philosophy or way of life.

 HUMANIST

"HAPPY MAN"

SYMBOL

ALTERNATIVE **13**

THE AIM OF YOGA

by Gopi Krishna*

Gopi Krishna was born in Kashmir in 1903. He is the author of three books and an activist in spiritual and social affairs. He believes that planted in man is a powerful reservoir of psychic energy, which when roused to activity can lead to transcendental states of consciousness, genius and supernormal psychic gifts. He is currently working on a Kundalini research project in Zurich, Switzerland.

Try to answer the following questions as you read:

1. From what is the word yoga derived and what does it signify?
2. How does asana relate to yoga?
3. What is the aim of yoga?

*Gopi Krishna, *The True Aim of Yoga*, **Psychic**, February, 1973, pp. 13-19. Reprinted with permission from **Psychic** and the author.

Broadly speaking, all systems of yoga in India fall into two categories, *Raja Yoga* and *Hatha Yoga*. Raja in Sanskrit denotes king, and Hatha means violence. Raja Yoga implies the kingly or easy way to self-realization and Hatha the more strenuous one. Both systems base their stand on the Vedas and the Upanishads; the main practices and disciplines are common to both.

In Hatha Yoga the breathing exercises are more strenuous, attended by some abnormal positions of the chin, the diaphragm, the tongue, and other parts of the body to prevent expulsion or inhalation of air into the lungs in order to induce a state of suspended breathing. This can have drastic effects on the nervous system and the brain, and it is obvious that such a discipline can be very dangerous. Even in India, only those prepared to face death dare to undergo the extreme discpline of Hatha Yoga. . . .

Yoga has its own value and importance. It combines a number of disciplines in an intense course of training with the aim of making spiritual enlightenment possible in the span of one lifetime. In India it is told that the human soul undergoes a long series of births and deaths, coming again and again into this world of happening and sorrow to reap the fruit of action done in previous lives. The cycle continues, with the practice of religious discipline, until one succeeds in cutting asunder the chain of cause and effect to reach the final state of union with the all-pervading, all-knowing First Cause of the Universe. . . .

The eight limbs of yoga are: *Yama*, which means abstension from all kinds of evil thought and deed; *Niyama*, which means daily religious observances, such as purity, austerity, contentment, study of scriptures, devotion to God, etc. The third is *Asana*, which means posture or, in other words, the most healthy and convenient way to sit for the practice of yoga. The fourth limb is *Pranayama*, which means the regulation and control of breathing. The fifth is *Pratyahara*, which means the subjugation of the senses to bring them within the control of the mind, a very necessary preparation for concentration. The sixth is concentration of the mind, known as *Dharana*. The seventh is *Dhyana*, which means a steady, unbroken concentration for a certain length of time or deep contemplation, and the eighth is *Samadhi*, which means the state of ecstatic or rapt contemplation of the inner reality.

It will thus be seen that yoga is more comprehensive and complex than is sometimes supposed. It is not only

Asana or posture, which is but a method to keep the body steady and straight when practising meditation. . . .

There are ascetics in India who can perform all the eighty-four Asanas to perfection and continue performing them all their lives, but they never attain to enlightenment. There are also ascetics who can suspend their breathing for days so that they can be buried underground or placed in hermetically sealed chambers for days and weeks without being suffocated. But despite such drastic measures, they often awake as one awakes from a deep sleep or a swoon without experiencing the least enlargement of consciousness or gaining any insight of a transcendental nature. This is called Jada-Samadhi, which means unconscious Samadhi. It is a kind of suspended animation similar to that of bears and frogs when they hibernate during winter. . . .

Interestingly, the word "yoga" is derived from the Sanskrit root *Yuj*, which means to yoke or join. Yoga, therefore, implies the union of the individual soul with the universal spirit or consciousness; according to all authorities, the final state of union with the divine is extremely hard to achieve. "After many births," says the Bhagwad Gita, "the discriminating seeker attains to me, saying all this (creation) is the Lord. Such a great soul is hard to find." According to the Tantras, out of thousands who take to Hatha yoga, hardly one succeeds. . . .

The aim of yoga, then, is to achieve the state of unity or oneness with God, Brahman, spiritual beings such as Christ and Krishna, Universal Consciousness, Atman or Divinity . . . according to the faith and belief of the devotee.

From the recorded experiences of Christian mystics such as St. Paul, St. Francis of Assisi, St. Teresa, Dionysius the Areopagite, St. Catherine of Siena, Suso and others, and from Sufi Masters including Shamsi-Tabrez, Rumi, Abu Yazid, al-Nuri, and al-Junaid, and from the experiences of yoga-adepts such as Kabir, Guru Nank, Shankaracharya, Ramakrishna, Maharishi Ramana to name a few, it is obvious that in the basic essential the experience is the same.

During the ecstasy or trance, consciousness is transformed and the yogi, sufi, or mystic finds himself in direct rapport with an overwhelming Presence. This warm, living, conscious Presence spreads everywhere and occupies the whole mind and thought of the devotee; he becomes lost in contemplation and entirely oblivious to the world.

104

The mystical experience may center around a deified personality such as that of a Saviour, Prophet, or Incarnation or around a Shunya, Void, or the image of God present in the mind of the devotee, or it may be centered on an oceanic feeling of infinite extension in a world of being that has no end. It is not merely the appearance of the vision that is of importance in mystical experience. Visions also float before the eye in half-awake conditions and in hysteria, hypnosis, insanity, and under the influence of drugs and intoxicants.

It is the *nature* of the vision — the feelings of awe and wonder excited by the spectacle that transcends everything known on earth. The enlargement of one's being, the sense of infinitude associated with the figure or the Presence and the emotions of over-whelming love, dependence, and utter surrender mark the experience and make it paramount importance as a living contact with a state of being which does not belong to this earth. . . .

Yoga signifies a momentary glimpse of ourselves, unfettered by flesh and the allure of the earth. For a short time we are invincible, eternal — immune to decay, disease, failure and sorrow. We are but drops in an ocean of consciousness in which the stormy universe of colossal suns, and planets looks like a reflection that has absolutely no effect on the unutterable calm, peace, and bliss that fill this unbounded expanse of being. We are a wonder, an enigma, a riddle; even those who have access to it some time in their lives cannot describe mystical experience in a way others can understand. For the soul belongs to another realm, another state of existence, another plane of being where our senses, mind, and intellect flounder in the dark.

Yoga also signifies the fact that this metamorphosis of consciousness is not only bone and flesh, but a thinking, feeling, knowing entity whose true nature is still hidden from the scholars of our age as it was hidden from the wise men of the past. Consciousness is something intangible, to our senses and mind. . . .

In order to be effective, yoga must be practised in the fullness of all its eight limbs or branches. Everyone who aspires to the supreme experience must strive for perfection; he must begin first with the development of his personality. . . .

Just as every atom of matter represents a unit of basic energy forming the universe, every human soul represents a drop in an infinite ocean of consciousness which has no beginning and no end. The average man, oblivious to his own divine nature and unconscious of his own majesty, lives in permanent doubt because of the limitations of the human brain. He is overwhelmed by uncertainty and sorrow at the thought of death and identifies himself with the body from the first to the last. He does not realize that he has a glorious, unbounded, eternal existence of his own.

All the systems of yoga and all religious disciplines are designed to bring about those psychosomatic changes in the body which are essential for the metamorphosis of consciousness. A new center — presently dormant in the average man and woman — has to be activated and a more powerful stream of psychic energy must rise into the head from the base of the spine to enable human consciousness to transcend the normal limits. This is the final phase of the present evolutionary impulse in man. The cerebrospinal system of man has to undergo a radical change, enabling consciousness to attain a dimension which transcends the limits of the highest intellect. Here reason yields to intuition and Revelation appears to guide the steps of humankind. . . .

The goal of yoga is this union with the universe of consciousness, enabling man to understand his origin and destiny in order to shape his life and the world accordingly. It is a herculean achievement, more full of adventure, risk, and thrill than the longest voyage in outer space. This is the greatest enterprise designed by nature for the most virile and most intelligent members of the race. . . .

"One who has attained to union with the Divine," says an Indian sage, "will not change his position even with a king," "That state is called yoga," says the Gita, "which having obtained one does not reckon any other gain to be greater, and established in which one is not disturbed even by great sorrow." Once again Jesus addressed the people: "I am the Light of the world. No follower of mine shall wander in the dark, he shall have the light of life."

"I am a king, O Sela", Buddha said to the Brahman of that name. "I am supreme king of the Law. I exercise rule by means of doctrine — a rule which is irresistible."

"In this state, that is the last state of love," says St. John of the Cross. "The soul is like the crystal that is clear and pure; the more degrees of light it receives, the greater concentration of light there is in it. This enlightenment continues to such a degree that at last it attains a point at which the light is centered in it with such copiousness that it comes to appear to be wholly light and cannot be distinguished from

106

the light . . . for it is enlightened to the greatest possible extent and thus appears to be light itself."

Christ and Buddha spoke but the truth. They were the Light.

ADVICE FROM ANN LANDERS

by Ann Landers *

Ann Landers, who is also Mrs. Jules Lederer, is a syndicated columnist for the Sun-Times Syndicate-Field Enterprises who specializes in giving advice to those who seek it. She has also authored **Since You Asked Me** and **Teen-agers and Sex**.

*Reprinted from **The Minneapolis Tribune** with permission from Ann Landers and Publishers-Hall Syndicate.

Dear Ann: In this age of conflicting philosophies, shifting standards and the emergence of what some choose to call The New Morality, please tell me how a person can differentiate between right and wrong.

Everyday I am beset by new conflicts. I'm frank to admit that I am utterly confused. Can you give me and others some words of guidance? — **Dark Side of the Moon**

Ann Says: Several weeks ago I heard a sermon by the beloved pastor of The Peoples Church of Chicago, Dr. Preston Bradley. He discussed this very subject and in conclusion quoted Dr. Harry Emerson Fosdick's six-point test for deciding right from wrong. I asked Dr. Bradley if he would send me his distilled version and he did so. Here it is:

Does the course of action you plan to follow seem logical and reasonable? Never mind what anyone else has to say. Does it make sense to you? If it does, it is probably right.

Does it pass the test of sportsmanship? In other words, if everyone followed this same course of action would the results be beneficial for all?

Where will your plan of action lead? How will it affect others? What will it do to you?

Will you think well of yourself when you look back at what you have done?

Try to separate yourself from the problem. Pretend, for one moment, it is the problem of the person you most admire. Ask yourself how that person would handle it.

Hold up the final decision to the glaring light of publicity. Would you want your family and friends to know what you have done? The decisions we make in the hope that no one will find out are usually wrong.

ABILITY TO EMPATHIZE

The ability to empathize, to see life and its problems through another person's eyes, is a skill you must develop if you intend to learn from the experiences of others.

Consider the following problem situation:

A CASE OF ADULTERY*

As the Russian armies drove westward to meet the Americans and British at the Elbe, a Soviet patrol picked up a Mrs. Bergmeier foraging food for her three children. Unable even to get word to the children, and without any clear reason for it, she was taken off to a prison camp in the Ukraine. Her husband had been captured in the Bulge and taken to a POW camp in Wales.

When he was returned to Berlin, he spent weeks and weeks rounding up his children; two (Ilse, twelve, and Paul, ten) were found in a detention school run by the Russians, and the oldest, Hans, fifteen, was found hiding in a cellar near the Alexander Platz. Their mother's whereabouts remained a mystery, but they never stopped searching. She more than anything else was needed to reknit them as a family in that dire situation of hunger, chaos, and fear.

Meanwhile, in the Ukraine, Mrs. Bergmeier learned through a sympathetic commandant that her husband and family were trying to keep together and find her. But the rules allowed them to release her for only two reasons: (1) illness needing medical facilities beyond the camp's, in which case she would be sent to a Soviet hospital elsewhere, and (2) pregnancy, in which case she would be returned to Germany as a liability.

*From **Situation Ethics,** by Joseph Fletcher, pp. 164-65. Copyright © MCMLXVI, by W.L. Jenkins, the Westminster Press. Used by permission.

She turned things over in her mind and finally asked a
friendly Volga German camp guard to impregnate her, which
he did. Her condition being medically verified, she was sent
back to Berlin and to her family. They welcomed her with
open arms, even when she told them how she had managed
it. When the child was born, they loved him more than all
the rest, on the view that little Dietrich had done more for
them than anybody.

When it was time for him to be christened, they took
him to the pastor on a Sunday afternoon. After the cere-
mony they sent Dietrich home with the children and sat
down in the pastor's study, to ask him whether they were

right to feel as they did about Mrs. Bergmeier and Dietrich. Should they be grateful to the Volga German? Had Mrs. Bergmeier done a good and right thing?

Try to imagine how the following individuals would react to this situation. What reasons do you think they would give for their actions?

A Legalist
A Situationalist
A Humanist
A Hindu
A Machiavellian
A Christian
An Atheist
You

SELECTED PERIODICAL BIBLIOGRAPHY

Because most high school libraries have a rather limited selection of books on the topics of philosophy and religion, the editor has compiled a bibliography of helpful periodical articles from 1963 to the present. Most school libraries have back issues of periodicals for at least a few years, and it is hoped that the following titles will be of some help to the student who is in search of a life philosophy.

Morris Adler	*What Is a Jew?* **Harpers**, January, 1964, p. 41.
Ian G. Barbour	*The Significance of Teilhard,* **Christian Century**, August 30, 1967, p. 1098.
Ernest Becker	*The Evaded Question: Science and Human Nature,* **Commonweal**, February 21, 1969, p. 638.
John C. Bennett	*In Defense of God,* **Look**, April 19, 1966, p. 69.
John Bird	*The Amish: 'We Want to be Left Alone',* **Saturday Evening Post**, June 17, 1967, p. 28.
C. Loring Brace	*The Origin of Man,* **Natural History**, January, 1970, p. 46.
Carin Burrows	*The Fierce & Erotic Gods of Buddhism,* **Natural History**, April, 1972, p. 26.
Marcia Cavell	*Visions of a New Religion,* **Saturday Review**, December 19, 1970, p. 12.
Commonweal	*The Cool Generation and the Church,* October 6, 1967.
Sarah Davidson	*The Rush for Instant Salvation,* **Harpers**, July, 1971, p. 40.
B.P. Dotsenko	*From Communism to Christianity,* **Christianity Today**, January 5, 1973, p. 4. (a conversion experience).
Theodosius Dobzhansky	*Evolution: Implications for Religion,* **Christian Century**, July 19, 1967, p. 936.
Vernard Eller	*The Mad Morality: An Expose,* **Christian Century**, December 27, 1967, p. 1647.
John T. Elson	*A Man for Others,* **Life**, May 7, 1965, p. 108. (concerns Dietrich Bonhoeffer).
Charles Fager	*Experimenting With a Simpler Life Style: An Interview With Harvey Cox,* **Christian Century**, January 6, 1971, p. 9.

| Joseph Fletcher | *Situation Ethics in a Changing Situation,* **Christian Century**, December 8, 1971, p. 1444. |

Mark Graubard — *Under the Spell of the Zodiac,* **Natural History**, May, 1969, p. 10.

Graham Greene — *On Becoming a Catholic,* **Commonweal**, September 3, 1971, p. 451.

Herbert Gold — *On Becoming a Jew,* **Commentary**, March, 1972, p. 949.

Kishi Hideshi — *The Religious Aspects of Cosmic Consciousness,* **Christian Century**, December 23, 1970, p. 1533. (a comparison of Teilhard de Chardin and Koyohiko Kagawa).

James Hitchcock — *The Christian and the Hippie,* **Christian Century**, August 16, 1967, p. 1040.

Joseph C. Hough, Jr. — *The Church Alive and Changing,* **Christian Century**, January 5, 1972, p. 8.

Robert Jastrow — *Cosmic Evolution,* **Natural History**, January, 1968, p. 32.

Morton T. Kelcey — *Is the World View of Jesus Outmoded?* **Christian Century**, January 22, 1969, p. 112.

Charles B. Ketcham — *The Search for the New Morality,* **Christian Century**, October 12, 1966, p. 1236.

Eugene Kinkead — *Is There Another Life After Death?* **Look**, October 20, 1970, p. 84.

John Kobler — *The Priest Who Haunts the Catholic World,* **Saturday Evening Post**, October 12, 1963, p. 42. (concerns Teilhard de Chardin).

John Kobler — *The Second Coming of Synanon,* **Saturday Evening Post**, February 8, 1969, p. 32.

Robert Kysar — *Toward a Christian Humanism,* **Christian Century**, May 21, 1969, p. 706.

John Lachs — *Dogmatist in Disguise,* **Christian Century**, November 16, 1966, p. 1402. (about Joseph Fletcher and the New Morality).

Life — *The Cult of Angry Ayn Rand,* April 7, 1967, p. 92.

Life — *An Empire Built on Sex,* October 29, 1965, p. 68. (concerns Hugh Hefner).

Life — *Paul Tillich,* November 5, 1965, p. 40.

David Little — *On the 'Ethics of Principle',* **Christian Century**, December 8, 1971, p. 1441.

R.J. McCauley & S.W. Fox — *Could Life Originate Now,* **Natural History**, August, 1968, p. 26.

John L. McKenzie, S.J. — *Lessons from History and Elsewhere,* **Christian Century**, July 8, 1970, p. 839.

John J. McMahon	*Catholic Students Look at Death,* **Commonweal**, January 26, 1968, p. 491.
Cary McWilliams	*Ethics in an Affluent Society,* **Christian Century**, June 22, 1966, p. 797.
Harold Martin	*A Vivid Portrait of the Famous Revivalist: Billy Graham,* **Saturday Evening Post**, April 13, 1963, p. 17.
John C. Meagher	*Creating a Christian Identity,* **Commonweal**, February 11, 1972, p. 439.
Watson E. Mills	*Glossalalia,* **Christian Century**, September 27, 1972, p. 949.
Robert Moskin	*Morality U.S.A.,* **Look**, September 24, 1963, p. 74.
Joseph B. Mow	*Jean Paul Sartre: Christian Theist?* **Christian Century**, November 23, 1966, p. 1437.
Newsweek	*Erik Erikson: The Quest for Identity,* December 21, 1970, p. 84.
Michael Novak	*Human First Christian Second,* **Christian Century**, June 19, 1968, p. 815.
Michael Novak	*What is a Liberal Catholic?* **Commonweal**, July 28, 1972, p. 398.
James Pike	*The Other Side,* **Look**, October 29, p. 43 and November 12, 1968, p. 50.
James Pike	*Why I'm Leaving the Church,* **Look**, April 29, 1969, p. 54.
William F. Pratt	*The Anabaptist Explosion,* **Natural History**, February, 1969, p. 8. (concerns the Hutterites and the Amish).
Elwyn L. Simons	*The Earliest Apes,* **Scientific American**, December, 1967, p. 28. (discusses which animals gave rise to the modern ape and man).
Elwyn L. Simons	*The Early Relatives of Man,* **Scientific American**, July, 1964, p. 50. (discusses the single stock from which man came).
Isaac Boshevis Singer	*The Extreme Jews,* **Harpers**, April, 1967, p. 55.
Lowell D. Streiker	*The Legitimacy of Rational Inquiry,* **Christian Century**, April 13, 1966, p. 458.
Donald K. Swearer	*The Appeal of Buddhism: A Christian Perspective,* **Christian Century**, November 3, 1971, p. 1289.
Time	*Astrology and the New Cult of the Occult,* March 21, 1969, p. 47.
Time	*Heretic or Prophet?* November 11, 1966, p. 56. (concerns Bishop James Pike).

Time	*The Hippies: Philosophy of a Subculture,* July 7, 1967, p. 18.
Time	*The Pursuit of Hedonism,* March 3, 1967, p. 76.
Time	*Is God Dead?* April 8, 1966, p. 82.
Garret Vanderkooi	*Evolution as a Scientific Theory,* **Christianity** Today, May 7, 1971, p. 13.
Frederick Wilhelmsen	*Catholicism Is Right, So Why Change It?* **Saturday Evening Post**, July 15, 1967, p. 10.
Christopher S. Wren	*An American Bishop's Search for a Space-Age God,* **Look**, February 22, 1966, p. 25. (concerns Bishop James Pike).

ACKNOWLEDGMENTS

illustration and picture credits

Page

6   (c) 1968 United Features Syndicate

10   From **The Great Dialogues of Plato,** translated by W.H.D. Rouse, edited by Eric H. Warmington & Philip G. Rouse, Copyright (c) 1956, 1961 by John Olive Graves Rouse. Reprinted by arrangment with The New American Library, Inc., New York, N.Y.

29   World Wide Photo
Ford Motor Company

30   Copyright (c) 1962 by The Billy Graham Evangelistic Association — used by permission.

47   Reprinted with permission from the Claredon Press, Oxford.

53   United Press International Photo

55   Designed by the editor and drawn by Steve Henning

86   Reprinted with permission of Llewellyn Publications, P.O. Box 3383, St. Paul, Mn. 55101.

90   Reprinted with permission of Llewellyn Publications, P.O. Box 3383, St. Paul, Mn. 55101.

101   The American Humanist Association

108   Reprinted with permission from Ann Landers and Publishers — Hall Syndicate.

MEET
THE
EDITOR

DAVID L. BENDER is a history graduate from the University of Minnesota. He also has an M.A. in government from St. Mary's University in San Antonio, Texas. He has taught social problems at the high school level for several years and is currently working on additional volumes for the opposing viewpoints series.